STRANGERS
AND
SECRETS

STRANGERS
AND
SECRETS

Communication
in the
Nineteenth-Century Novel

R. A. York

Rutherford ● Madison ● Teaneck
Fairleigh Dickinson University Press
London and Toronto: Associated University Presses

Associated University Presses
440 Forsgate Drive
Cranbury, NJ 08512

Associated University Presses
25 Sicilian Avenue
London WC1A 2QH, England

Associated University Presses
P.O. Box 338, Port Credit
Mississauga, Ontario
Canada L5G 4L8

The paper used in this publication meets the requirements
of the American National Standard for Permanence of Paper
for Printed Library Materials Z39.48-1984.

Library of Congress Cataloging-in-Publication Data

York, R. A., 1941–
    Strangers and secrets : communication in the nineteenth-century novel / R.A. York.
        p.   cm.
    Includes bibliographical references and index.
    ISBN 0-8386-3533-4 (alk. paper)
    1. English fiction—19th century—History and criticism.
2. Communication in literature.   3. Outsiders in literature.
4. Secrecy in literature.   I. Title.
PR868.C636Y67   1994
823'.809355—dc20   92-55125
                                                                          CIP

CONTENTS

STRANGERS
AND
SECRETS

INTRODUCTION

This book arises from two convictions: first, that the quality of our lives depends very much on the quality of our communication with other people; and second, that the novel is a particularly important literary form because it specially focuses on the quality of communication and on the problems of communication.

The first of these two points may not look at all original. Many modern philosophers and sociologists, such as Mead and Vygotsky, claim that communication with other people is precisely what gives us a personality, and the importance of communication is one of the commonplaces of our times; complaints about "the impossibility of communication" are hackneyed, and a crude belief in maximizing communication can become a substitute for real thought about what makes relationships worthwhile and how far self-respect and individual personality depend on ordering and codifying communication. It is when the stress is placed on the *quality* of communication and on the problems inherent in any concern for authentic communication— for honest, appropriate, effective communication—that the real significance of the topic emerges; and that concern for authentic communication is precisely what many of the great novels are concerned with, including many of the great novels of the nineteenth century, from Jane Austen to George Eliot. This book, then, aims to bring out the ways in which novelists have highlighted what is at stake in communication, and it hopes to show two things: first, what the modern reader can learn through seeing such works as a reflection of the way people talk to each other (or write to each other, or convey feelings and attitudes through bodily actions); and second, how novelists, using language in the course of a simulated contact with a reader, produce a richly self-conscious and self-questioning texture by reflecting on how this fictitious contact relates to practical contact between people.

Such questions, of course, are studied by many people other than novelists, notably linguists, sociologists, psychologists, and communication theorists. The study of sociolinguistics has special relevance to the novel. In this introduction, I sketch out some ideas which have been formulated by such theorists and which I hope may help to define some of the effects gained by literary writers. We must avoid the sense that novelists are only illustrating theories (and we should especially avoid any impression that this book contains the ultimate theory to which literary authors have been paving the way); it is rather that the imaginative sensibility of novelists has discerned in social reality a set of issues which may also be approached more systematically—if less intensely and with less sense of the total coherence of life in society—by theoretical or scientific means, and that the theoretical formulations may help us to clarify our perceptions and to see more readily the similarities between the concerns of the past and those of the present.

The first point to stress is the necessity of communication. If we are with another person, we are obliged to communicate, in some way, whether it be a casual offhand nod or an articulate conversation. The starting point of any social contact is a sense of some sharing of experience, however minimal; it may be only the recognition of the other person's presence. One aspect of this minimal obligation much treated by novelists (and by playwrights) is what is called *phatic communion* (i.e., communion by speech); we are obliged to speak even to people to whom we have nothing to say, and therefore we find ourselves obliged to talk trivially. An obvious example is our daily casual remarks about weather. Many people feel this is futile or disturbing, because they contrast such talk, which has no purpose beyond itself, with what they take to be the true purpose of communication, namely to present interesting information or opinions, and feel that any talk which has no such content is an affront to human thought. Such trivial talk can be presented in fiction for amusement or mockery, or as a source of frustration and boredom. Here is a serious problem for the novelist: literature normally claims to be considered as significantly new information, structured to exclude the inertia and predictability of much practical language. Yet much of the novelist's material, being drawn from everyday prose, is essentially banal, redundant, entropic. And it is a serious challenge for the novelist to make the banal into the basis of something new.

The degree of repetitiveness of speech of various characters can also become a matter of literary concern. Few of us totally escape redundancy in our everyday language, because our need to communicate may exceed our inventiveness; but it can be significant that certain characters are conspicuously repetitive in their speech, while others are much less so—and narrators, on the whole, not at all. Character, it quite often seems, consists precisely of redundancy in speech.

Our disquiet at banality and redundancy is symptomatic of our more general readiness to judge communication in various ways. We can find some aesthetic interest in communication: we can admire the elegance, originality, ease, sophistication, and ingenuity of speech or gesture. We can start to produce speech and gestures with aesthetic qualities in mind, hoping to enrich our contact with others by such qualities of display or theatricality, by the manner of communication as well as by the content. We also can apply moral criteria to communication, judging other people and ourselves in terms of decorum, honesty, respect for convention, or respect for other people in social interchange; we can impose a kind of restriction on what people say by the threat of disapproval or by more direct penalties: ultimately, perhaps, by the threat of imprisonment or other legal punishment for morally or politically subversive speeches or publications. The feeling that one's words or significant acts are in some way censored is common in characters in nineteenth-century novels, and much psychological interest and narrative tension arise from their attempts to come to terms with such feelings, all the more so because they may well themselves believe that expression should be controlled.

Next we should note that communication has various possible sorts of content. We communicate information, of course; perhaps that is what the word "communication" most readily suggests to some people. But we communicate many other things, too, not always as consciously. We communicate attitudes, for instance. Sometimes we deliberately indicate our respect or dislike for the person we are talking or writing to; but very often we communicate such feelings incidentally or unknowingly. We "betray" our feelings, through choice of vocabulary, tone of voice, even the direction of our gaze and the arrangement of our limbs. This has been much studied by communication theorists such as Giffin and Patton or Rossiter and Pearce, who have helped us to become aware of things in our own conduct of which we may not have been cognizant previously, and have stressed how far such signals of attitude very between different cultures. Both increasing self-consciousness and variety of cultures are two of the main concerns of the nineteenth-century novel.

A very important dimension of this is the way we use other people's manner of communication to categorize them as being either "like us," "one of us," "our sort of person," or not; in particular we may respond to dialect, to forms of language which indicate regional or class origins, but we also respond to speech rhythms, pitch of voice, choice of topic, politeness levels, habitual gesture, clothing and appearance, and many other clues. This reveals that we communicate things involuntarily—especially things concerning social standing. Such unintentional communication is a major part of our everyday lives and is acutely noted by many novelists.

Linguistic variation is the major topic of study of sociolinguistics. (For a thorough and enlightening modern account, see Downes 1984. Good collections of essays on linguistic variety are Bailey and Shuy 1973, and Fillmore 1979. There are useful comments on the use of linguistic variety in fiction in Page 1973, and in Leech and Short 1981.) The major aspects of variation that are usually identified are those of dialect, register, and individual variation or idiolect.

Dialect is variation of language between speakers defined in terms of social groups. People most readily think of variation between geographical groups, and therefore they speak of a Yorkshire dialect or a Wessex dialect: dialect comedy is normally an exploitation of this sort of variation. But there also are class dialects: what some people call standard English perhaps would be better described as the dialect of the educated classes of Southern England.

Register is variation according to occasion; thus while any one person will normally speak only one dialect, he or she may use many registers. People use different vocabulary and syntax, even different pronunciation, volume, and pace according to whether they are speaking about commerce or football; whether they are speaking face to face, using the telephone, or preaching a sermon; or whether they are conversing with close friends or strangers. Register is of vital importance in the novel as it is in social life, because it implies a certain linkage between linguistic form, occasion, and purpose of utterance: it takes for granted that there is a way of talking about a certain situation—which implies a particular attitude to it and may suggest a certain pattern of relationships between the people who are involved in talking about it—a pattern which is taken to be inherently right. If, like Casaubon in *Middlemarch*, some one talks about marriage in the vocabulary of ceremonious religious obligation, then marriage *is* a matter of religious obligation—for you and, unless there are objections, for the person you are talking to. Of course, people can object to the way someone talks about a topic; they may think it too frivolous, too technical, too easily based on a sense of superiority to the speaker's interlocutors: but it is much more difficult than objecting to the content of what he or she may say, because the objection to content can be done in the same register, while challenging the register appears to be a fundamental disruption of the shared social activity of talking. Choice of register is already an interpretation of a situation, and such interpretations can be misguided, perverse, or arbitrary; examining such tacit interpretations is one thing that novelists can do in their presentation of communication.

It seems natural to assume that there is a dimension of personal or individual variation in addition to these purely social variations. We certainly recognize in ordinary conversations that our acquaintances have particular speech habits (frequent use of certain words, for instance, or of certain syntactic structures, characteristic speeds, or intonations); literary stylistics had been dedicated largely to the study of individual styles of authors, and it has done so with considerable success. It might seem that if such variation is truly individual, it will escape the scope of sociolinguistics, and that if it presents any communication problems, they will be different from those that have been indicated in these pages. Two answers can be made, though tentatively. First, individuality is itself a social matter. It is part of our social training that we admire people who are prepared to "be themselves," which may include choosing an unusual style of utterance. But this unusualness itself will be defined against a social norm shared with an individual's hearers; and there certainly will be cases where the choice of deviant forms is itself a deliberate theatrical self-display, a demonstration of a command of the forms of a language, even the less used ones, and of readiness to contradict the conventions that make them less used. Second, it may well be argued (and some examples from the novels discussed in this volume will support this view) that what we call individual style is often simply a habit of using particular registers, or of performing certain kinds of speech act, even when the particular register or act is not obviously appropriate. Thus people who address their partners in conversation by name with abnormal frequency are characterized, as speakers, by a high—possibly an excessive—concern with the act of making contact, which is itself a perfectly normal speech function.

However satisfying such explanations of individual variation might be—and they certainly call for much more investigation than this introductory chapter can give them—the fact remains that there is individual variation, and that it is one more thing that can make people aware of the differences between themselves and the persons they speak to, differences which need to be negotiated in dialogue and which may seem to be a danger to communication, as well as a source of fruitful complementarity.

Another important aspect of communication is the range of speech acts that people perform. Much of their communication is neither fact nor attitude; it is an act, calculated to produce some effect on the listener or reader, some change in him or her; they give orders or warnings, persuade, entertain, threaten, or promise; they perform official or ceremonial functions such as marriages, award ceremonies, and job appointments (cf. York 1986). Such things are important because they imply a whole social setting and a commitment to some sort of social role; people can only give orders if they are in some position of superiority. They can only warn if they genuinely believe in some danger; they can promise only if they intend to live up to the promise. Moreover, these acts only work if the person addressed recognizes that they have the right to perform them, through their superiority, genuine belief, good intentions, and the like. In these ways, language reveals a lot about the way people live with other people, and the novelist's depiction of speech acts demonstrates the way people accept or rebel against the codes that govern their relationships to others.

The previous paragraphs have often referred to "language," but they also have mentioned nonverbal communication, through significant acts or gestures. I hardly need stress the importance of spoken and written language, given its central role in education and culture, except to stress the fascination many authors have with correct naming, their sense that language gives a direct awareness of the essences of reality, and to emphasize their awareness of the way characters are revealed by their use of style and rhetoric, or by their choice of register or conversational strategies.

Recent theorists have drawn attention increasingly to nonverbal communication—to the way we respond to facial expressions, eye contact, gestures, bodily position, distance from others, arrangement of seating. Sometimes they claim that what is conveyed in such ways is even more important than what is conveyed verbally, both because it is perceived as more truthful and because it affects matters of attitude and belonging which are fundamental to the way we deal with people. Victorian novelists were well aware of these questions, and the way in which the nonverbal can conflict with the more rational forms of verbal communication is often a source of fascination and concern in their work.

Another important question is that of the medium of communication. Many people tend to think of face-to-face interaction as the characteristic form of communication, and this is widely depicted in fiction; but there are many other less direct means of communication (although fewer in the nineteenth century than there are now, in our age of telephone, video, and computer links). We may communicate by letter or—most intriguingly for the novelists—through intermediaries (who are placed in a difficult position in which they speak partly for others and partly as themselves); and such indirectness of communication can raise impediments or uncertainties.

This in turn raises the question of the effectiveness of communication. Although some people may be inclined to refer, perhaps unconsciously, to a model of communication in which some message simply passes intact from one person to another, this is not what happens. In fact, people produce words or gestures which, explicitly or implicitly, invite a certain interpretation; if all is well, the person receiving the communication will provide precisely that interpretation. But things rarely go that well; even the most acute partner, in the most favorable conditions, may get a slightly different sense of the message, and very often incomplete contact, ambiguous or misleading phrasing, preconceptions on the part of the listener, viewer, or reader, inability to recognize the appropriate context, or other such factors may lead to misinterpretation, speculation, or complete misreading. Such confusions are a familiar part of daily life (more for some people than others, no doubt); they are very much part of the stuff of fiction.

If we try to identify a single concern which is at the base of these varied problems concerning communication, it would be a concern with *otherness*. Any communication implies some degree of difference between the communicator and the person being addressed: at the very least, the person being addressed does not already have the information being provided; more often there are differences of class, gender, nationality, disposition, religion, moral attitude, and so on.

At the same time, communication implies similarity: at the very least the person addressed normally has the same language as the communicator (if not, both parties have to find a shared code of gestures); again there is a whole range of personal and social features which may be shared. It seems reasonable to suppose that easy conversations are those where much is shared, but that conversations where there are great differences between the interlocutors, where each is specially conscious of the otherness of the person he or she is with, may be the most stimulating. This certainly is the view that is implied in many of the novels considered in this work. That is why they often are concerned with strangers and secrets, with people who join a community from outside and therefore fit ill into the accepted patterns of conversation and communication, and with blocks to communication brought about by discretion, politeness, shame, intrigue, and self-interest. Communication is interesting when it is difficult, when it is a challenge and leads people to become aware of what they are capable of achieving in communicating with others and of what obstacles they have to overcome to deepen their contact with others. This is not to say that the novelists simply prefer the strange to the familiar. On the contrary, the choice between them is often the subject of acute consideration.

The outsider is a type of character who allows the novel to foreground the problems of social exclusion and the ensuing self-awareness that is perhaps less acutely felt by a great many people in the modern world. The types of figure who can fulfill the role of outsider will be recognized readily enough, and fictional cases will not be difficult to think of. They include the foreigner, the exile, the solitary, the socially mobile, the intellectual, the child, the innocent (the latter is the absolute outsider: a person who appears alien to all cultures). It may be that the importance of the bastard and the foundling in the novel should not be explained psychoanalytically, as Marthe Robert suggests (Robert 1972) but sociologically; these exceptional biological situations inevitably carry with them exceptional, exterior social positions. One important social result of this interest in unorthodox family relations (Said 1984, 117) is that the principle of inheritance is often obscured or endangered in novels, threatening both the economic order of the fictional world and the continuity of moral and emotional life within it. The importance of the outsider in the novel is like the importance of the stranger in society, brilliantly analyzed by the sociologist Simmel: the stranger brings to a society an objectivity, compounded of "distance and nearness, indifference and involvement"; he is seen as a representative of common humanity, beyond the restrictions of specific society, restrictions which his mere presence therefore highlights (Simmel 1964, 404–5).

The outsider in the novel may be an observer or a learner (as in the great tradition of the *Bildungsroman*); he may disrupt the routine by crime or scandal (the importance of scandal as the matter of fiction is very properly stressed by Grivel 1973, 275); the contact of society and outsider may be seen in terms of a fear of contamination.

There is one novel that brings out these relationships with exceptional clarity: Thomas Mann's *The Magic Mountain*. Hans Castorp, the innocent, the outsider because he is healthy in a world of sickness, comes to the tuberculosis sanatorium on the magic mountain of Davos to see, at first with surprise and ridicule, its eccentric regime, its routines of death and dissolution; in it he finds a microcosm of the conflicting ideologies of Europe, Communist and Christian, rational and passionate, and from being at first an amused observer, finds himself contaminated, quite literally with tuberculosis, and metaphorically with thought, passion, and self-awareness. It is by no means difficult to find such themes, tautly interwoven, in many other novels, and not least in the nineteenth-century English novels that this study will be considering. In *Wuthering Heights*, for instance, Lockwood is an outsider who discovers the bleak and inhospitable unchanging routine of Wuthering Heights, is largely eager to differentiate himself from its "uncivilized" directness, but gradually finds himself contaminated by sexual attraction and by curiosity at Mrs. Dean's stories; Heathcliff has been an outsider who has learned to comprehend the ways of life of the Heights and Thrushcross Grange—and not least to be aware of their differences, who has sought to maintain himself separate, as a voice of immediate natural passion, and has eventually let himself be contaminated by gentility and thoughtfulness.

One very prominent theme in fiction which relates to this contact with the outsider is one I call, a little approximately, the opposition of exogamy and endogamy. Strictly speaking, exogamy, in anthopological terms, is the obligation to marry outside one's own clan, while endogamy is the obligation to marry within it. There is no such formal obligation in European society, but people do feel it significant that they can choose as a sexual partner either the outsider, the person who brings novelty into the social group, or the familiar figure, the family friend, the near brother—and novelists often heighten this opposition by insisting that the central character go through a process of uncertainty and temptation before making the final choice. The choice of endogamy, in this sense, is a choice of redundancy; it is a reaffirmation of the known social world and of the character's original place within it but with some change, because a novel could hardly exist without change. The choice of exogamy is one of adventure, of the new, of oneself as capable of change, of communication with the new. Any sort of dialogue, it may be argued, involves change in both participants (Jourard 1968, 161): the novel, insofar as it is centered on the ethics of communication, assesses that change, and endorses or limits it.

Novels are not only about strangers; they are often about secrets, about interrupted and distorted communication, about hidden and suppressed facts. The significance of this is immense: such restrictions of communication delimit an area of special value or sensitivity for the characters; the nature of these sensitive areas is a major social factor, and it changes in history, from a socially precarious betrothal in *Emma* to a murder in *Middlemarch;* and the curiosity we feel as readers (which is not totally alien to curiosity felt in real life, as apparent, for instance, in much newspaper reading) is a testimony both of our respect for the fact of secrecy, for the value of the vulnerable or the illicit as a private possession too important for public knowledge, and of our impatience with it; it suggests a feeling that the *real* self of the other person lies precisely in his or her unwillingness to tell us everything. The sociological importance once again is clear: Simmel implies it strongly when he speaks of secrecy as "one of man's greatest achievements," as a "possession of privileged knowledge"—which entails the conception of privilege, of knowledge as having value, which is perhaps one of the chief things that the novel as a genre seeks to establish and to examine—and of the "fascination of betrayal" (Simmel 1964, 330–33).

Betrayal is important because the very delight of secrecy brings with it a fascination with wresting away the secret, with gaining access to the withheld knowledge. This explains the love shown by many novelists for "scenes," in the sense of unduly public emotional display, for revelations, voluntary or involuntary, for eavesdropping. Eavesdropping is "a transformation of secrets and secret telling . . . a reflection of story-telling culture in which the contrast between public and private forms an important element" (Vernon 1984, 87).

Indeed, the whole of the novel may be thought of as a sort of eaves-dropping (Vernon 1984, 93); the reader is a Peeping Tom who is allowed to see and hear more of the characters than they themselves know of each other. A beautiful example appears in the scene in *Adam Bede* where Hetty Sorrel stares at herself in a mirror. She is alone: her satisfaction and self-absorption would be disapproved of by the world of morality and work in which she spends her public life; the glamour of sensual self-awareness is captured from a dull background of propriety, and so must be secret. But she is not quite alone; the reader is with her, and shares, in part, that sensual delight.

This cult of secrecy is a form of a dichotomy often used in thinking out our social and personal values, the division between public and private. The growth of this distinction, the creation of an area of life which is not accessible to most other people, the feeling which becomes deeply ingrained in people throughout their earliest training in family and school that there are some things that are not done or said in public, is often thought to have most deeply contributed to the whole historical growth of personality as such. N. Elias, especially, has studied the "civilising process," precisely in terms of an increase in such discriminations, on the levels primarily of bodily restraint and of restraint of violence through political order. By restricting sexuality to the sphere of the family and violence to the order of the state, by suppressing direct demonstrations of emotion and concealing certain zones of the body, by putting a veil of shame between the social classes, Western civilization has created a *homo clausus*, a human being shut off from his like, for whom the "true self, the core of individuality" is the restrained impulses which are hidden from all others (Elias 1978, I: 258).

Privacy, it is often claimed, has grown in recent years with the increased concern of people for the family unit that goes with prosperity, good housing, easy transport, and a consumer economy; it has even been regarded as creating a religion that has modified or supplanted the heritage of Christianity (Luckman 1967). It is not quite paradoxical, perhaps, that it has also been argued recently that privacy is now decreasing (Perlman 1968, 25); this latter view regrets the diminution of an older, more radical sense of privacy as difference, as choice and eccentricity. The consumer-based privacy which is now normal in most of our society, is a privacy of uniformity, in which what is at stake is not what one chooses to do or the kind of person one chooses to be, but the right to live uninterrupted and unobserved.

What has the novel to do with such issues? The answer lies in the different ways experience can be presented within a fictional work. Because dialogue in fiction can be so organized as to show the private purpose through the rules of the social game, and because the narrator can pass readily from external "objective" presentation of characters and their publicly observable speech and acts to internal "subjective" presentation of their purposes and emotional responses, the novel can expose with special force and lucidity the tension of which we are all conscious between what we feel ourselves to be and to want and what we expect other people to see us as. The novel turns the tension into spectacle: it thus allows both a release from tension and an enlightened comprehension of the tension.

These matters have been the subject of a great deal of subtle and meticulous analysis in the theory of the novel. Readers may be referred for an extremely sound, pertinent, and economical account to the work of Shlomith Rimmon-Kenan (1983). Among the large number of important contributions to the topic one may also mention those of Bal (1977), Cohn (1978), Fowler (1977), Genette (1972, 1983), Prince (1984), and Uspensky (1973).

A number of points are particularly relevant in the perspective being advanced here. First, there is the concept of point of view. The concept is complex and has perhaps not been entirely eluciated. In essence, it is that the events of a story may be told—at any one moment or consistently—in terms of the knowledge available to a particular character and of the understanding and judgment of that character. It will be seen that these aspects of the issue already raise many possible degrees of participation in the character's consciousness. It is especially important, as Genette has insisted, to distinguish the presentation of the facts as known to a character from the presentation of them through the type of language that is associated with that character.

The latter type of presentation is what Leech and Short call "discoursal point of view" (Leech & Short 1981, 272); it amounts to giving the character the right to tell the story, virtually supplanting the narrator. This discoursal point of view is close to free indirect discourse, (i.e., indirect speech not explicitly signalled as such) which enables a character's thoughts or words to be presented without obvious distinction from the voice of the narrator (Banfield 1982, 11,89;

cf. Pascal 1977). It should be noted, however, that free indirect discourse itself does in many uses imply an author's voice indirectly, because it is recognizable as such by its oddity, and therefore by the irony the author must be assumed to be directing toward it (Rimmon-Kenan 1983, 113).

Complementary to such techniques of delegating storytelling to the characters, ironically or seriously (which of course also include the possibility of sections of the narrative being openly undertaken in the first person by one of the characters of the novel), there is a whole range of techniques, more or less subtle, by which authors can show their endorsement of the information provided by the characters and their interpretation or judgment of it. Quite often, novels tend toward a resolution in which an unchallenged truth is proclaimed; the conclusion of the novel often seems to attain a state of openness, naturalness, universality, and obviousness, a state of revelation which transcends the conflicts and obscurities of communication that prevail in much of the body of the text. For this to be achieved, it is necessary that there be some harmony at least between author, or narrator, and character, despite the multiplicity and dissonance of languages that novels normally tend to show (which have been most strongly emphasized by the critics associated with Mikhail Bakhtin). Such harmony can be indicated by repetitions of terms from the character's utterances in the words of the narrator, by the adoption in the character's speech of specially rhetorical forms, by his adoption of moral criteria not previously articulated, by an increased abstraction or generality, by changes of pace and rhythm, by expressions of approval and admiration on the part of other characters, or even, most austerely and most elusively, by the simple cessation of irony. We find little difficulty in a certain kind of film in recognizing the moments when the hero and sage stares into the camera and pronounces the judgment of the director—through sophisticated viewers may receive such judgments with more detachment than the film perhaps demands. The corresponding moments in novels have their own signals, and in major novels they are perhaps rarely possible to locate with absolute certainty. The point is an important one; such moments of certainty might give a single focus to the novel and imply a dichotomy between the true vision of the narrator and the more or less false visions of the characters; they might build authority into the text. But we often like to feel that there is some freedom of perspective in the text and some respect for the views and sensibilities of (some of) the characters; the rightness of the narrator—the authority of his language—must, to this extent, be held in check.

Conversely, the author can indicate that speeches should not be taken as conveying a truth or a valid judgment or interpretation, but as symptomatic or exemplary of a certain state of mind, which may be shown to have effects in the development of the plot, or in the patterns of sympathy created in the text. If a speaker is preoccupied with remarks about money, it is likely to be because the author is characterizing him as a miser and intending to show the results of avarice in the plot; if he speaks with excessive passion of his beloved, it may be because he is being characterized as too trusting or sensual, and so as preparing the doom that meets the passionate. False languages and their implications can be part of the web of the plot; the challenge to readers may lie in requiring them to judge—with more or less explicit guidance in the text—which languages are held, within a particular work, to be false. And it should be remembered that obviously false languages are likely to be of fairly little interest; the novelist deals, very frequently, with plausible false languages, with the fascination of error.

To summarize: the novel is a form which depends on mediation of language. We are interested, as readers, in the voice of the characters, in the view of life in general, and of the events of the novel in particular that they can offer us by means of that voice, in the relationships between their sensibility and their language. But we are not directly exposed to that language (as we are in drama or in much poetry); we come to it through the perspective of a narrator. Narrators often differ from their characters. Often they are different in social terms: they are very likely to be middle-class intellectuals, whereas the characters may very often not be (if predominantly middle-class in the Victorian novel, they are rarely intellectuals in any very fully developed sense). Even if no such differences of permanent status arise, there is an inbuilt difference in perspective on the events of the novel, because the characters are participants, while the narrator is normally a mere observer. (If the narrator is a participant, there is very often a gap in time between the events and their narration which introduces this same possibility of detached observation, which is, however, eliminated in certain special forms that have been popular at certain times in history, such as the diary-novel, the epistolary novel, the novel composed of stream of consciousness.) One of the great dichotomies that is used for making sense of experience in our civilization is that between the spontaneous and the reflective, or in Schiller's terms, between the naive and the sentimental. It is a dichotomy virtually inherent in the novel, in which the narrator is almost bound to be sentimental, to present matter for reflection, analysis, and judgment, while the characters are more or less naive, acting out of the immediacy of their needs and desires. The narrator's reflectiveness is what most pervasively determines the reader's response, no doubt; but it may be the characters' vitality in action and speech that makes for the essential attraction of the novel.

The relation of narrator to character, then is complex, made of harmony and dissonance. The same may be said of the relation of narrator to reader, though the point is perhaps more delicate to establish. Harmony and dissonance, manifest in variety of language, affect a wide range of social activity and may relate to differences: of class and culture, in the way people read particular situations, in energy or reflectiveness, or in the complexity or individuality of personality. The following chapters seek to show in more detail the way these complexities are used by the English novelists of the nineteenth century to constitute rich and varied images of social life as contradiction and as collaboration, and of personality as secrecy and as communication.

1

EMMA

> What really matters in the work of any writer is not the degree or kind
> of referentiality or content. Rather it is the writer's moral relation to
> language. The overriding concern of Jane Austen's novels—and of many
> of her heroines—is the nature of true utterance. (Tanner 1986, 6)

There is, in the work of Jane Austen, a constant concern with the
difficulties and dangers of communication. The essential concern of
Sense and Sensibility, the first mature novel, is with the repression of
information, of guilty and embarrassing knowledge, with the feared
contagion by speech of a corrupt sexuality, and with the way that
sexuality is purged through a series of confessions, reluctantly admitted by the heroine—who, for all that, is constituted above all as a
character by her acceptance of other people's intimacy. In *Mansfield
Park*, there is the constant opposition of the unspeaking heroine
Fanny Price and the theatrical tempters, Henry and Mary Crawford.
The heroine of *Persuasion*, the last completed work, feels an insecurity in the face of "the sort of necessity which the family-habits
seemed to produce, of every thing being to be communicated" (83)[1]
(the awkwardness of phrasing is itself symptomatic of an unease in
speech). *Persuasion*, too, contains two of the most powerful and sympathetic scenes in the author's work, and they are scenes of displaced
communication. In one, a strained and sparse conversation between
the heroine and her former lover falls into silence; the two are separate; but suddenly the lover steps forward to lift off her small nephew
who has insisted on climbing onto her back. Physical proximity replaces verbal intercourse. In the other, the two are again separate:
the lover is writing a letter in silence, while the heroine holds a
conversation, apparently of general import, with a common friend;
the lover realizes that her talk of constancy in love is pertinent to
their own situation, but he does not intervene in the conversation,
he does not speak to her: he adds to the business letter he is writing

a personal letter for the heroine, which he gives her as he leaves. It proves to be an eloquent and persuasive declaration of his constant love. The written word replaces the spoken word; private communication is disguised as public communication.

In general, *Emma* is less tense than this. Communication is less constantly a matter of anxiety and indirectness which is one reason why *Emma* is one of Austen's most charming and welcoming books. But the concern is still there, and that is one reason why it is one of her most ambitious books.

The world of *Emma*, in fact the society of Highbury, is a world, on the whole, of extraordinary ease of communication. Nearly everyone is fluent; people are rarely at a loss for what to say. It is a world in which ease of communication is prized, where "a well-bred ease of manner, and a readiness to talk" (190) are signs of gentlemanly status, where a "handsome letter" (18) is a topic of general discussion (even if it can be judged by a more discriminating reader as merely "a fine flourishing letter," 148). It is a world of civility, as is Austen's world in general. Civility does not go quite unchallenged, even among the rank and file of Highbury: to the excessive good humor, sociability, and civility of Mr. Weston is counterpoised the malevolent incivility of Mr. John Knightley, with his hatred of any social gathering and his love of domestic inertia. John Knightley, admittedly, is something of an outsider; the sixteen miles from his London home are a real social distinction, and his brusqueness and teasing clearly go too far at times. But he is, after all, closely related to the hero of Highbury society, Mr. George Knightley; and domestic inertia is a value held quite seriously in much of Jane Austen's work. It is a value incarnated, to the point of caricature, by Mr. Woodhouse, whose valetudinarian affability is regarded with affectionate respect throughout the village.

But one does not have to be the misanthropic John Knightley to see something wrong with Highbury's civility. The ease or speech of village life goes with an undiscriminating acceptance of things, which the novel clearly does not endorse. Emma, though certainly a figure of excessive discrimination, is surely right in regretting Mr. Woodhouse's lack of taste, in wishing he had "a little less of openheartedness" (320). The whole village, in her eyes, lacks distinction, and barely escapes vulgarity—vulgarity being the one inelegance excluded by Highbury's tolerance. The narrator, though more acceptant than Emma, is aware of the dangers of a mentality in which nothing is significant because everything is equally important: Mr. Woodhouse, fortunate in his "total want of taste" (362), is an image of a society in which nothing is too trivial to say or to repeat. Thus he feels no shame in his constant expressions of pity for those more fortunate than himself ("Poor Miss Taylor!"), in his frequent appeals to the wisdom of Mr. Perry the apothecary, in his regular praise of the panacea, gruel. Harriet Smith feels no shame (though Emma does try to instill it) in her frequent over-circumstantial and syntactically monotonous accounts of life at school or of the customs of the Martin family. The sameness of this world is perhaps most clearly illustrated in the conversation between Mr. Woodhouse and his elder daughter Isabella: well trained by him, she has her own concerns about health and her own favorite apothecary. The conversation of the two is like a conversation of mirrors. The effect for the reader is brilliantly funny; but it is disturbing, too, because it reduces human contact to a recital of the foreknown. Interchange, in fact, hardly matters: this is a society of monologuists.

There also is a ritual of conversation; as in other works of the author, people "talk by rule" (91; cf. *NA* 25); so here, too, on formal occasions especially, they play their part, and the narrator observes with a discreet irony. Thus Frank Churchill is "accused of having a delightful voice, and a perfect knowledge of music; which was properly denied; and that he knew nothing of the matter, and had no voice at all, roundly asserted" (227). The denial is a proper one, and Austen never doubts the need for such propriety; but the mechanical correspondence of accusation and defense suggests a language too formulaic to offer much satisfaction or much sense of the ingenious games-player that Frank Churchill really is. Such is the "trivial communication and harmless gossip" (21) of Highbury, such is the "common routine of acquaintance": what is elsewhere more harshly described by the narrator as "every day remarks, dull repetitions, old news and heavy jokes" (219).

These banal utterances are, moreover, in a sense impersonal. No one possesses them. So there are speeches, quoted or summarized by the narrator, which are attributed to no one: they represent the sort of thing that people say. It is accepted with only minor caution that things "get round" or "get about" (327, 417; cf. 185), and they get around with astonishing speed. Before he can inform Emma of Mr. Elton's marriage, Knightley is forestalled by Miss Bates; bracing herself to tell Harriet the shocking secret of Frank Churchill's engagement, Emma finds she has been told by Mr. Weston. "These matters are always a secret," Mr. Weston comments, "till it is found out that every body knows them" (468). Overhearing is rife: the scene in which Miss Bates holds a noisy conversation with Knightley through her window, leading even the mild Jane Fairfax to comment with some irony when Miss Bates attempts to repeat the content of the conversation, that "we heard his kind offers, we heard everything" (245), is a parody of the accessibility of utterance that prevails in Highbury (just as Knightley's contribution to the conversation has been a parody—though a kindly one—of the niceness, the ready approval that Highbury expects for everything).

But this ease of language has its price. First of all, it depends on a restriction: on a limitation of subject latter to the concrete reality of what happens in Highbury, on an elimination of "delicate subjects" (in the particular case, Mrs. Weston's humble origins as a governess, 201), on avoidance of the distressing, the intimate, and the hostile. Money and marriage are the centers of conversation; beyond that there is the private. Hence the need to avoid eclat, to behave well by not showing emotion, to fear what might be reported of one, for instance by letter writers spreading Highbury gossip to Ireland or Maple Grove (368). The narrator, of course, knows more than the villagers; he has an ease in handling abstract terminology, in generalizing and judging, that few of the characters share. This skill in using language is perhaps nowhere displayed more openly than in the introductory portraits of some of the characters: few people in Highbury could speak with the narrator's confidence of Mr. Weston's "active cheerful mind and social temper" (15). There is an ease of psychological assessment that links the narrator with the reader over the heads of the characters. And yet in other ways, the narrator shares the characters' limits. He too never goes outside Highbury, to narrate Frank Churchill's London haircut, to meet Mrs. Churchill or Captain Campbell, those remote figures of power; he shares the characters' sense of place and absence. In some ways he is actually more restrictive than the characters; if their kindliness makes them democratic enough to accept the Coles, the narrator is not democratic enough to report Mr. Coles' conversation; if they are patient enough to hear Mr. Knightley's farming talk, the narrator is not patient enough to record it. If they have daily contact with Mr. Perry, the narrator only lets readers see him once, and then through the eyes of Emma: he is "walking hastily by" (233) as if to preserve his peripherality in the text.

Second, conversation in Highbury depends on outsiders. Life without strangers would become moribund (Monaghan 1980, 116; 1981, 111). This highly homogeneous world needs something alien, something different to talk about: news is a commodity eagerly sought. Novels, of course, require novelty; they require events; *Emma* shows that this need may be at least a little awkward. The reader may be, if anything, rather relieved when Mrs. Elton's much respected connections, the Sucklings, fail to arrive in Highbury, but for the inhabitants this is a frustration: "no such importation of novelties could enrich their intellectual stores at present" (352). One novelty who has been imported, of course, is Mrs. Elton herself. She is eagerly awaited, an object of curiosity and speculation, her role almost written for her before she arrives. To that extent, she isn't so much of a novelty; she's what a vicar's prosperous bride must be.

Her coming brings problems, too. She acts with familiarity before she has really become familiar; she has the admired ease of conversation, but for one native of Highbury at least she has "too much ease" (270) and it soon becomes "licentiousness" (284). She even gets on to Emma's "delicate subject," much to Emma's disgust. Her weaknesses are blatant, especially in the domain of nomenclature: "Knightley," "Jane Fairfax," and especially her husband, who becomes "Mr E," "my lord and master," "my caro sposo" (or on one specially regrettable occasion "caro sposa"), and who reciprocates by repeatedly calling himself "an old married man." Emma, at her engagement, is to be much more circumspect about naming. Names matter. They imply a decorum which is at odds with a certain self-displaying facility of speech. But the infringement of decorum is what makes for the vivacity of the novel, and even for its resolution, because Mrs. Elton's disrespect for Knightley is one factor in focusing Emma's attention on him and because her manipulation of Jane Fairfax is one thing that leads Jane's relationship with Frank Churchill to a crisis. The novelist perhaps rejects vulgarity as Emma clearly does; but she relies on it, too, for variety, energy, and stimulation.

Highbury, as we have seen it so far, stultifies language, and with it, social interchange. Much of the interest of *Emma* for the reader lies in its presentation of the public futility of social life, a presentation which is often very funny, sometimes (especially with Miss Bates) tenderly patient and aloof at the same time, sometimes painful in its sense of waste and restriction. But this is not the whole of Highbury. Highbury has the fortune to be incarnated in someone better than itself, its "general friend and adviser" (58) Mr. Knightley. Mr. Knightley is associated with Mrs. Weston, who in his own judgment is rational and unaffected like himself (13) (on the "rational" in *Emma*, see Stewart 1968). He largely shares Highbury's sense of language: tactful, decorous, hardly less concrete in vocabulary than his neighbors, excluding the private hardly less rigorously. He is a distinguished man, to be sure, because he is capable of disapproval. His readiness to judge often produces discontinuities in the novel. As early as chapter 5 of volume 1, for instance, the chapter starts brusquely in mid-conversation with Knightley disapproving Emma's friendship for Harriet Smith. Beyond that, it is a capacity which often gives rise to a neat Austenish wit, as when he comments that his sister-in-law always thinks like her husband, "except when he is not quite frightened enough about the children" (40), and more often, especially in his reproaches to Emma, to a sober rhetoric of parallel phrasing and rhetorical questions, signs of rationality made conspicuous. Once at least it leads to a forceful abstraction on linguistic principle: defending, in a properly balanced way, Mrs. Elton's use of language, he defines what propriety amounts to: "Mrs. Elton does not talk *to* Miss Fairfax as she speaks *of* her. We all know the difference between the pronouns he or she and thou, the plainest-spoken among us; we all feel the influence of a something beyond common civility in our personal intercourse with each other" (286). Mrs. Elton perhaps refutes this defense of her by speaking *to* him of his "peculiar sort of dry, blunt manner" (356). But perhaps she confirms his view; the outrageousness of this indicates precisely that speech cannot be uncontrolled.

Besides, Mrs. Elton has truth on her side. Knightley's manner is blunt, or to use the term that he prefers, plain-speaking; he speaks directly, his words are sincere, natural, unadorned; they are "plain, unaffected, gentleman-like English" (448). As a lover, he verges on the inarticulate. He is a judge of style; conscious enough to recognize that "one man's style must not be the rule or another's" (445), he is nevertheless clear in recognizing the function of style in flattery or ingratiation and does little to mitigate his condemnation. In some respects, Knightley is not a man of speech at all; sparing with words, he is effective in action. The point is made, almost as in a parable, in the episode of the coach. Finding that he has, unusually, arrived at a party by coach, Emma congratulates him on coming "as you should do . . . like a gentleman." Knightley neatly replies that had she not seen his arrival, she might not have discerned him to be more of a gentleman than usual; she is judging him, he implies, superficially, "by my look or manner" (213). But this remark is a suppression of the truth, which is that he uses his coach not for gentlemanly display but for gentlemanly service: he wants to put it at the disposal of Miss Bates and Jane Fairfax. The act is one of "unostentatious kindness" (223); unostentatious precisely in that action excludes comment.

Knightley's language, in short, is one of effectiveness. And here lies a paradox of the novel. Much as author and narrator appear to admire this language, it is not one they can use. (Knightley, Tanner neatly points out, would not have written *Emma*, 1986, 201.) If the narrator's language shares with Knightley's a serious moral vocabulary, it nevertheless is differentiated from it and from that of the other characters, precisely by not being directly effective and by not being a rhetoric. How, then, can the voice of the narrator contain wholehearted praise of the voice of her hero? The issue emerges in the coach example: the author wishes to praise Knightley's supression of a fact, but can only do it by arranging for revelation of that fact.

More generally, the narrator has to remain at a distance from Knightley. At times, it is true, Knightley's voice and consciousness are the voice and consciousness of the book; most notably perhaps in his suspicion of Frank Churchill: "He feared there must be some decided involvement. Disingenuousness and double-dealing seemed to meet him at every turn. . . . It was a child's play chosen to conceal a deeper game on Frank Churchill's part" (348). The narration passes discreetly from a summary of Knightley's feelings, through a sentence which may report his own words in free indirect discourse ("seemed to meet him"), to conclude with one that definitely does so. The distinction of narrator and character is suppressed. This is an effective example of the integration of indirect speech with narrative of which Page speaks and of the way it can silence the author's voice (Page 1972, 134–36), or at least displace it, because by the end of this passage it is Knightley who is conveying to readers a forceful statement of the author's ethos of language, her condemnation of a double language, of a hidden game; and who better than Knightley could convey it? The text gains in authority from the rectitude of the character. But it also gains something else: uncertainty. The true condemnation of duplicity arises as suspicion. The narrator cannot yet inform the readers that Frank Churchill actually is duplicitous or what form his duplicity will take. To do so would lose narrative tension, and it would deprive readers of a direct experience of the need to decipher puzzling signs. Much of the novel is about the misreading of signs; readers have the chance to misread them for themselves.

But if the narrator occasionally bestows on Knightley this solemn status as the voice of general truth and of particular speculation, almost always Knightley is seen from outside. At least once, the narrator makes his distance from Knightley quite ostentatious; Mr. Knightley, he comments, "for some reason best known to himself," has taken a dislike to Frank Churchill. Later the reason is revealed: it is jealousy with regard to Emma. Here, for the time being, Kinghtley is the locus of a partly opaque inner life. But on the whole, we do not know him to have any inner life distinct from his outer self or from his public speech and action. We do not know of his having any plans with regard to Emma (or to Jane Fairfax or Harriet Smith). He has no deeper game. Only after his proposal to Emma do we discover that he has loved her for some time—and suppressed his love. To have hidden purposes and give clues to them, as Frank Churchill has done, is duplicitous; to suppress one's purposes and give no ground for comment even to a kindly narrator reduces to a minimum, it seems, the inner life—if the inner life is a hidden one—and is proof of authenticity. The contrast of private and public, of display and secrecy that critics have stressed in Austen's work is acutely present in much of *Emma* (Butler 1975, 264; Monaghan 1980, 159). Mr. Woodhouse, Mrs. Elton, and Harriet Smith show no difference at all between outer self and inner self; Emma, Frank Churchill, and Jane Fairfax show the difference more or less acutely (Emma because the narrator sees within and through her; the others because he doesn't). Mr. Knightley shows the inner forcibly reduced so he can guarantee the consistency of the outer. Secrecy, obviously, makes for seriousness in this novel. Those who have no secrets make an entertaining spectacle, but those who do have secrets call for respect, sympathy, judgment, fascination. Civility is the law of the society depicted, and it is a real law, a norm really referred to. But privacy is the center of the novel's imaginative concern.

Emma, herself, does have civility. She is part of her society. She shares—usually—its kindliness, tact, and decorum, its sense of what

cannot be said. Her attraction for readers is in part due to this conformity with a good-natured environment. She shares, too, some of
the less appealing aspects of Highbury life: the thirst for news, the
readiness for "half an hour's uninterrupted communication of all
those little matters on which the daily happiness of private life depends" (117). Even her arch-opponent Mrs. Elton offers an image of
how far Emma belongs to her world, as Mudrick points out (Mudrick
1968, 194; see also Fergus 133, 1983; Monaghan 1980, 131); their love
of controlling others, specifically of having protegées, and perhaps a
certain liking for display, for admiration, for cultivation of a self-
image, their readiness to regard themselves as equal to anyone, their
concern for distinction, link them surprisingly.

   But Emma certainly thinks of herself as different from Highbury.
Distinction, in fact, is one of her great concerns; her excessive and
inexact sense of class-distinctions is one sign of this; another is her
hostility toward Jane Fairfax, based initially on fear that Jane might
seem to be too much like herself. To a great extent she really is
different. If the normal voice of Highbury is that of banality, and
Knightley's that of a mature orthodoxy, Emma's is one of opposition
and innovation. She is, in Tanner's terms, a force against inertia, and
so disposes of a wider range of discourse than any other character
(Tanner 1986, 181, 199). To this extent, she is an instance of the
language of consciousness as defined by Banfield (Banfield 1981, 41),
a language constituted by its difference from everyday speech. She
likes to generalize, excessively: "I know that such a girl as Harriet
is exactly what every man delights in—what at once bewitches his
senses and satisfies his judgment (64). She likes paradox: "A lucky
guess is never really luck. There is always some talent in it" (13).
She likes contradiction, as in almost all her conversations with
Knightley, till his proposal. She likes to speak of herself; Mrs. Weston
is lucky not to have to please two people, "especially when *one* of
those two is such a fanciful, troublesome creature" (10). She likes
hyperbole: "A young farmer, whether on horseback or on foot, is the
very worst sort of person to raise my curiosity" (29). Her syntax is
more complex than that of most other characters, her sentence
rhythms more varied; her vocabulary is wide and she often discusses
the application of items of vocabulary. She parodies the style of Mr.
Elton, Mrs. Elton, and Miss Bates. Whether she speaks "playfully"
or "exclaims" or "cries," her speech clearly is fully controlled and
consciously adapted to her partners: she modulates her style percepti-

bly in speaking to Mr. Woodhouse, Mrs. Weston, Knightley, Frank Churchill, and it would not be excessive to say that this a theatrical style, and quite the reverse of Knightley's plain speaking.

The effect is, largely, to isolate her: her father, we are told early in the novel, "could not meet her in conversation, rational or playful" (7). A good deal of the entertainment of the novel—and a certain measure of embarrassment, as well—comes from Emma's cool coping with unequal partners in conversation, including her father, Harriet, Miss Bates, and Mrs. Elton; and the crux of the story lies in her choosing between two people who are her equals in conversation, though in different ways: Frank Churchill and Knightley.

This confident mastery of social speech has its limits, as does the banal facility of Highbury in general. First, it leads to a dishonorable excess of communication, as she herself realizes after she betrays to Frank Churchill her suspicions about Jane's relationship with Mr. Dixon, and as she is forcefully made to realize when she can't resist betraying to Miss Bates her view of her tedious ramblings. She is wrong about Jane Fairfax and more or less right about Miss Bates; but what matters is that suspicion and contempt are private matters which must be cut off from public utterance.

Second, it means that the public Emma is largely constituted by other people. Often she does not initiate speech or action but responds aggressively to other people's initiatives: Mr. Weston is thought to be happily unmarried, so Emma will marry him off; Mr. Woodhouse is against marriage, so Emma offers to find a wife for Mr. Elton; Harriet is delighted with the Robert Martin family, so Emma judges them socially unacceptable; Highbury expects to like Jane Fairfax, so Emma rejects her with stiff distaste. And when Emma does undertake something, as with her series of projects for Harriet, the result is catastrophic. It appears that, for Jane Austen, the sort of self-conscious, deliberate individualism that Emma stands for is false; it often is little more than a negative image of an undistinguished norm.

Third, Emma's surety in explicit communication does not extend to indirect communication. *Emma* is largely the story of what Emma calls her "blunders" (after amusing herself at the comic spectacle of other people's blunders). She misreads signs conveyed by others: Mr. Elton's assiduous attentions are not meant for Harriet but for Emma herself, Frank Churchill's occasional moments of hesitation and hinting are not signs of increasing attraction to her, but of his real preoccupation with Jane. And she gives false signs herself: Mr. Elton is quite reasonable in thinking that her warm encouragement is meant to invite his suit. Open speech is controllable and an instrument of control, but the meanings that arises from manner and implication escape Emma's conscious ordering.

In such instances, then, there is a gap between explicit statement and assumed meaning, which relates to the fourth major limitation of Emma's social speech: that it is remote from her inner speech. The public Emma is teasing, self-assured, active; the private Emma, though no less articulate and certainly no less rhetorical, is given over to calculation, speculation, and self-reproach. Is this, for instance, recognizable as Emma? "The young man had been the first admirer [of Harriet Smith], but she trusted there was no other hold, and that there would be no serious difficulty on Harriet's side to oppose any friendly arrangement of her own" (31). The moderately complex syntax, the nice triple balance of rhythm, the abstraction of vocabulary, the reference to herself, the euphemistic view of the "friendly arrangement," with its discreetly chosen epithet—this is the public Emma. But the depersonalization of definite articles ("the first admirer"), the vocabulary of opposition ("serious difficulty", "oppose") and of calculation ("she trusted"), the symmetry that opposes, through the pivotal "but," an admitted fact to an intention: these are signs of a private effort of thought that Emma does not speak aloud. Emma's public theatrical self is almost a mask; at best it is a very partial and indirect reflection of her inner self.

This inner self provides the consistency or most of the novel. A paradox of *Emma* is that it largely endorses Knightley's values (cf. Liddell 1963, 116), but that it sees most things through the different language of Emma. Often it does so to endorse Emma's vision: when, for instance, "Emma felt the bad taste of her friend" (54), readers need not doubt that Harriet's bad taste is real (indeed, they should have felt it already). At other times the narrator openly reprimands Emma: recounting the cause of her initial dislike for Jane Fairfax, he comments, "These were her reasons—she had no better" (167). But most often he simply reproduces—largely in free indirect discourse—Emma's observations and responses. Many of these will prove to be unfounded. Hints may have been given of their unfoundedness, as in the contrast between Emma's suspicions of Jane Fairfax and the much more positive attitude toward her of the narrator and Knightley. But the hints are not yet conclusive; much of the time, the novel's fascination is that of an intelligent uncertainty. Emma interests readers, even charms them, because of her self-awareness, her tact and sensitivity, her alertness, and most of all, perhaps, because of her mistakes. She is an "imaginist" (335); the imagination of the novelist enters into her imaginations with curiosity and concern, but also with lucid detachment; it shows that an active imagination uses ingenuity, boldness, and close attentiveness, and that it is fundamentally irresponsible.

If the division of inner and outer is one of the things that make for Emma's interest and weakness, it is most strongly incarnated not in her but in the two strangers whose coming to Highbury makes the major action of the novel, whose novelty stirs up the inert society of the village, who are an object of talk even before their arrival and a source of news ever after it, whose impact eventually leads (through Knightley's jealousy) to the satisfying resolution of Emma's marriage: Frank Churchill and Jane Fairfax. Strangers bring secrets, deception, and duplicity. And it is not just the harmless tactful suppression of the private that is discreet and normal, but an acute divisive secrecy that threatens social trust and so the reliability of communication. The discovery of the secret engagement of Frank Churchill and Jane Fairfax near the end of the novel resembles the disclosures of sexual impropriety that bring about the denouement of *Sense and Sensibility*, *Pride and Prejudice*, and *Mansfield Park*. It brutally brings to light a private life that has threatened, disturbingly at times, to disrupt the even flow of public life with which it seems incommensurable; and the disclosure, the expulsion of the scapegoats, in Girard's sense (Girard 1981; though here a kindly, forgiving expulsion) allows the installation of a society of intimacy and sincerity in the form of an appropriate marriage.

Frank Churchill and Jane Fairfax share between them the two sides of a deceptive division: he is all outside, she is all inside. Is there here some half-conscious traditional view of the characters of men and women? Perhaps so; but certainly there is a foregrounding of a contrast of appearance and reality which is essential elsewhere in the book: the couple of Emma and Knightley restates the dichotomy less painfully and with a different emphasis (not outer vs. inner, but divided vs. coherent).

Frank's language is one of pure sociability: he adapts himself superbly to his interlocutor, as with his sorrowful assurance to Mr. Woodhouse that "a thoughtless young person will sometimes step behind a window-curtain, and throw up a sash, without its being suspected. I have often known it done myself" (252). He is polite, deferential, appreciative, persuasive; as handsome in language as he is in person. He is not far from fulfilling Emma's prediction, made before his arrival: "To you, he will talk of farming; to me, of drawing or music; and so on to every body, having that general information on all subjects which will enable him to follow the lead, or take the lead, just as propriety may require, and to speak extremely well on each" (150). This is Emma's myth of agreeableness, proffered almost as a parody, at least as provocation, to the less flexible Knightley, who castigates her ideal as "the most insufferable fellow breathing!" And it proves that Frank Churchill really is the myth come true; in him, *Emma* is a display of surface, but not quite a "triumph of surface" (Mudrick 1968, 205). When at the end of the novel Emma recognizes a resemblance between herself and him, she is recognizing her own superficiality, her own existence as appearance.

Jane Fairfax, on the contrary, has grave difficulty with language, and is intriguing for that reason: "She is a riddle, quite a riddle!" Emma exclaims (285)—and readers may well agree. She is silent (to a degree not entirely explained by the volubility of her aunt Miss Bates); she is reserved, "disgustingly, . . . suspiciously reserved" in Emma's view (169); and she confesses herself, in the general access of explicit and truthful self-knowledge that constitutes the climax of the novel, that she has been "so cold and artificial! . . . I know that I must have disgusted you" (459). If she speaks forcefully and coherently, it is in a strange, disproportionate, and inappropriate way: her outbursts about the importance of letter writing and of postal deliveries (which anticipate Anne Elliott's excessive readiness to talk about ships and the navy in *Persuasion*) show more obsession with communication than skill in it (and the obsession remains inexplicable till we realize that her absent correspondent is Frank Churchill; communication, for her, seems to be a function of absence) and her normal conversational style has a stiffness and caution that hints at some repressed intimate sense. Thus her reply to Frank's apparently gossipy and cheerfully spiteful observation about the Eltons' meeting in a public place: "I was only going to observe, that though such unfortunate circumstances do sometimes occur both to men and to women, I cannot imagine them to be very frequent. A hasty and imprudent attachment may arise—but there is generally time to recover from it afterwards" (373). Obviously the theme of disparity between public life and intimate feeling, so frivolously, touched on by Frank, has disturbed her: this strained language, with its periphrases, careful verbs of intellectual evaluation, meticulous pairing of complementary terms, periodic structure, and repeated antithetical form is an exercise of the will in controlling expression.

What, then, is the relationship of Frank and Jane? We hardly know, because the narrator barely shows it. He chooses, primarily, the viewpoint of Highbury, and shows the couple through the consciousness and conversation of his characters (especially through Emma). He does confirm the general view that Frank Churchill is handsome, but it matters more that he should be thought to be handsome. With Jane Fairfax the situation is a little more complex: soon after her arrival is announced, the narrator brusquely starts a chapter (chapter 2 of book 2) with a summary of her life so far. For once he moves in space outside Highbury, and in time to a period before the events of the story; the specialness of Jane Fairfax, the pathos and extraneity that make her an object of fascination, are manifest. But this is a partial account, and he shows us so: "her account to her aunt contained nothing but the truth, though there might be some truths not told" (166). The untold truth is her relationship to Frank, and it remains untold through much of the text.

We see of it what Highbury sees: a displaced and ambiguous communication, carried on through looks not meant to be public, remarks with a double sense, an excessive familiarity with local gossip, and snatched moments of company which reveal themselves as silent scenes of non-communication. And we learn of the misunderstandings that disunite them, that are brought to an end not by their will but by the death of an absent character, the quarrels about how public their relationship can be. This is what strangers bring to Highbury: a sense of the problematic character of communication, of the tension of public and private, of the deviousness of signs. The game of anagrams, the jumbled letters that make up a blunder, is not just child's play: it conveys a deeper game—on the author's part.

How does Emma react, to this and to her own misreadings? She gradually attains self-knowledge and the speech in which self-knowledge can be authoritatively constituted. Her inner debates and self-reproaches mature, especially as she acquires Knightley's vocabulary of reason and feeling, till finally, in a crucial passage, she endeavors "to understand, to thoroughly understand her own heart" (412). The style is at once agitated and complex: parallel questions and exclama-

tions, hesitations and climaxes, anxious reformulation of concepts—
all pick out this moment as the language of conversion. The conversion is a rewriting of the past; and when Emma and Knightley, after
their engagement, attain an intimate language together, it proves
again to be concerned with retelling their previous relationship.
Emma will further recapitulate the past with Frank and Jane (though
we do not see these two together again after the disclosure of their
love: open sincerity between *them* is inconceivable). The culmination
of the novel is a discovery of what happened during it.

Readers may have an inkling of the proper reading of the past
already. It has already been inscribed in the narrator's stance at two
points. One is the ball at the Crown, when Knightley is presented
through Emma's eyes, with "his tall, firm, upright figure among the
bulky forms and stooping shoulders or the elderly men," his gentle-
manlike manner and natural grace: a fit rival, at the least, for Frank
Churchill (326). Knightley is a physical being, for Emma; he is not
just the voice of rightness. The other sign of Emma's love for
Knightley is her view of Donwell, with its "suitable, becoming, characteristic situation, low and sheltered—its ample gardens stretching
down to meadows washed by a stream, of which the Abbey, with all
the old neglect of prospect, had hardly a sight—and its abundance
of timber in rows and avenues, which neither fashion nor extrava-
gance had rooted up" (358). As Elisabeth Bennet falls for Darcy in
viewing Pemberly, so Emma is loving Knightley in loving Donwell,
and is a fit mistress for the estate. The narrator takes his cue from
her in describing the land as he talks of the "considerable slope,"
with its "steeper form," and the "bank of considerable abruptness
and grandeur, well clothed with wood" (360). Character and narrator
are at one in feeling the orderliness of place: a shared sensibility
which is a tribute to the owner of the place.

The latter passage aptly praises continuity, because the novel ultimately chooses to endorse an unchanged world. The story is made
possible by the intervention in Highbury of strangers, but it is con-
cluded by a restoration of what has already existed: hence the retro-
spective language of the conclusion. This novel is not, like many
novels, about the pursuit of desire; it is about the recognition of
desire. In choosing the reality of Knightley against the appearance
of Frank Churchill, or nature against art, Emma chooses permanence
against change, development against incident. Above all, perhaps
she chooses endogamy against exogamy (Knightley is not quite her

brother, we recall). Jane Austen was clearly seriously concerned that sexuality conflicts with family affection. The theme of the outsider is recurrent in her work (Liddell 1963, 107); it is a crucial component of the "instability of desire, language and society," which is a paradoxical condition of the propriety to which her novels aspire (Miller 1981, ix). Her other novels show the conflict of desire and family in different forms. *Pride and Prejudice* shows the domestication of the alien object of desire (alien to place and in class); here, then, is a union of lovers which involves a violation of social differences (Banfield 1981, 41). But this is hardly typical; *Mansfield Park* shows the elimination of the alien and the transmutation of fraternity into marriage. *Emma* follows *Mansfield Park* in this: it asserts that the strange, by disturbing the conditions of communication, makes the familiar knowable, non-banal, and desirable.

Note

1. References in the text are to J. Austen, *The Novels*, ed. R. W. Chapman, 5 vols. Unless otherwise indicated, references are to *Emma; PP* indicates *Pride and Prejudice; NA, Northanger Abbey;* and *P, Persuasion*.

2

WUTHERING HEIGHTS

Isabella Linton has been showing signs of ill health. Her sister-in-law, Catherine, the principal heroine of *Wuthering Heights*, "peremptorily insisted that she should get to bed; and having scolded her heartily, threatened to send for the doctor." Isabella responds by complaining of Catherine's "harshness." Catherine, "amazed at the unreasonable assertion," twice queries the word "harsh," and a third time after Isabella's explanation, which is that she had been excluded the previous day from a conversation between Catherine and her childhood companion, Heathcliff. Finally Catherine offers to repeat the whole conversation, and Isabella refuses.

> "I don't mind the conversation", she answered: "I wanted to be with—"
> "Well!" said Catherine, perceiving her hesitate to complete the sentence.
> "With him; and I won't always be sent off!" (141)[1]

Stylistically, the passage is not a specially prominent one. It serves largely to introduce the forceful and rightly much quoted speech in which Catherine characterizes Heathcliff, with the mixture of accuracy and passion that typifies her treatment of him, as a man marked by violence, ambition, and devotion to herself. But the introductory passage already contains much that is fascinating, precisely because it is unremarkable in the context of the novel as a whole. In style, there is the habit of identifying and judging speech acts by adverbs such as "peremptorily" or "heartily"; by the choice of verb, "exclaim," "cried," or "sobbed"; by adjectives such as "unreasonable." There is the obsessive and polemic repetition of key words, such as "harsh," "yesterday," and "conversation," and the intensity of synonymy or near-synonymy, as with "losing your reason," "Is she sane?", and a little later, "madness"; or, in a single speech, "walk,"

40

"ramble," "sauntered." There is the plethora of exclamations, imperatives, and appeals; the shifting of rhythm in a convincingly captured conversational manner, contrasting Isabella's fragmentary and immature complaints with Catherine's more poised, relaxed, and coherent defense. In particular, there is the incomplete sentence ("to be with—") by which Isabella momentarily dominates the discussion, as she requires her nearer to ask for completion before Isabella can produce her culminating act of determination, and betrays her barely controlled passion for the unnameable Heathcliff. In what is revealed of the relationships of the characters, there is the conflict of an uncompromising wish for attention with an uncompromising wish for evasion—though the latter is expressed in livelier, less obviously self-centered, and more varied terms. There is the fact that this is a discussion about a discussion, and the fact that the events complained of took place the previous day and so can hardly be amended now. Both characters are ready to reproach and abuse each other in the strongest terms, to attribute motives to each other without foundation, to defend themselves with over-meticulous rhetoric. This is like much of the dialogue of *Wuthering Heights;* it is childish bickering raised to the level of genius.

Where does the genius lie? Partly in persistence. In a novel which focuses largely on the theme of unrelenting passion, the novelist is unrelenting in her depiction of antagonistic dialogue. This is true both in the sense that a very large proportion of the dialogues in the novel, until the final chapters, are like this one, and in the sense that each dialogue tends to be presented as almost static; there is an excess, a malignant exuberance of language, as the conversation keeps saying the same things in new words or in the same words. Feelings are few and precious to those who hold them: Isabella's longing confronts Catherine's aloofness. But words are many; they are the product of an ill-channelled energy whose fluctuations and sudden impulses are conveyed in the hesitations and expansiveness of the speakers. The genius also lies partly in the text's astounding combination, rather suggestive of Dostoevski, of truthfulness and extremity: the querulousness and the brutality go beyond what most readers probably experience in their daily intercourse, but readers will nevertheless recognize the strategy of conversation, the rather tangential replies, the awkward attempt to cope with a difficult interlocutor by choice of tone, the yielding to irritation in the face of obstinacy. But the genius also lies in the theme which is approached here, and which is inherent in the strangeness and the lucidity of language, in its overexplicitness and its futility, a theme which is debated implicitly or openly through much of the novel and makes for much of its tension and seriousness: the theme of the value of language.

Isabella "doesn't mind the conversation": what she wants is presence. At a first approach, the point is simple enough: having a conversation recounted is no substitute for participating in it. Few lovers (and this is where we discover that Isabella is in love with Heathcliff, or "infatuated" in the more pejorative term of the narrator) would be content to be told what their beloved has been saying. But why not? This passage actually puts the question in fairly hyperbolic terms, for Isabella does not merely feel the personal force of Heathcliff as distinct from feeling interest in what he may have said, or as an enrichment to what he may have said. She does not see presence and words as complementary and proceeding alike from a coherent personality; she sees presence as other than words and superior to them. What is at stake here as in much of the novel is possession of a person. Heathcliff is being disputed between his permanent love, Catherine, and the alien Isabella. It will prove that he cannot really be possessed, as some other characters can; but the aspiration is still there at this stage.

Isabella's conception, furthermore, contaminates the whole text of the novel. Readers are not allowed to mind the conversation in question, the content of which is never recounted, or for that matter many other of Heathcliff's utterances. He is a taciturn character, anyway, and the narrators quite frequently present his speech in such forms as this: "I found him very intelligent on the topics we touched" (50), or this: "he said precious little, and generally the truth" (79). The narrators suppress his voice in favor of his effect on themselves or others (and so reveal something about the hearers: Lockwood, the first narrator, the sophisticated Southerner, admires his intelligence and ease; Nelly Dean, the serious Northerner, admires his truthfulness and discretion). What does he say, what does he think, what does he talk about? These things quite often remain outside the scope of the story, which, however, is dominated by his presence.

The mystique of presence perhaps relates to the view that Catherine, at least, treats Heathcliff as a Hegelian essence, as self-contained and independent of social relationship (Eagleton 1975, 102), though she might not have chosen such terms herself. It goes with a mystique of the name, which is often treated as if it contained in itself some intangible quintessence of personality. Lockwood is first inveigled into fascination with the Wuthering Heights story by discovering Catherine's name (in various forms) written on a shelf in his bedroom: the name is soon fleshed out in a horrifying nightmare. In the passage first discussed, Isabella doesn't venture to use Heathcliff's name; in a conversation with her husband shortly after, Catherine interrupts him when he gets as far as "Heath—" (165). Informed of Catherine's death, Heathcliff "endeavoured to pronounce the name, but could not manage it" (203). Hearing that his own son by his marriage to Isabella is called Linton, the name of Isabella's family which he regards as having deprived him of rightful possession of Catherine, he observes "They wish me to hate it too, do they?" There is magic in names and a sort of taboo about them: to name is to evoke not any one quality or act of the person, but his or her very self.

The immediate effectiveness of presence, without communication, can be malignant. Heathcliff speaks significantly of the fear he has inspired in his son Linton: "since then, my presence is as potent on his nerves, as a ghost" (318). Ghosts prove crucial to the book, which begins with Lockwood dreaming of Catherine's ghost and ends with the ghosts of Heathcliff and Catherine apparently being seen together. Ghosts are significant precisely because they don't need to communicate; being there is enough for them. The major symbol in *Wuthering Heights* for unqualified presence, in fact, is death. The point is made in a violent speech by Catherine to her husband in which she speaks of her intended grave as "my narrow home out yonder— My resting place where I'm bound before Spring is over! There it is, not among the Lintons, mind, under the chapel-roof; but in the open air with a headstone, and you may please yourself, whether you go to them or come to me!" (165). The speech anticipates the end of the book, with the narrator contemplating the three headstones, placed side by side in a ghastly parody of adultery, of Catherine, Edgar Linton, and Heathcliff; and it brings out the significance of the placing. Death is a choice of location, an assertion of home; Catherine asserts nature against the Lintons, culture, and religion, and she imposes a choice on Edgar (it is obvious that Heathcliff would choose nature against the Lintons, if indeed he had the choice). The presence of these three to each other in death is an overcoming of the separation or division much feared and much suffered throughout the novel: it seems to be possible precisely because they can no longer have anything to say to each other and so contrasts, in tense irony, with this speech which attributes meaning to that propinquity. The speech, like so many of the speeches in *Wuthering Heights*, and especially of Catherine's, is an expression of indifference and chosen isolation. It constitutes a challenge to Edgar to define his own identity as a Linton and thus alien to Catherine, who is a child of the less prosperous and sophisticated Earnshaw family of Wuthering Heights itself, or else as her husband. To choose the latter, as Edgar finally does, is to be an act of acquiescence to her imperious will. Will, Leslie Stephen noted (Stephen 1970, 100) seems to have a "royal prerogative" in this book; its language often bears witness to the fact, and not least on the lips of Catherine.

A choice of permanent presence is a choice of identity. Identity is conceived in class terms (Thrushcross Grange as against Wuthering Heights), hence the importance of the "specific and informed socio-logical content" to which Mrs. Leavis draws such sympathetic atten-tion (Leavis 1969, 97) and to which Winnifrith has devoted some perceptive pages (Winnifrith 1973, 189–94). But it also is conceived in metaphysical terms (culture as against nature). We shall see that these contrasts prove in the course of the book to be less than clear-cut (cf. Eagleton 1975, 107, 113), but they are nonetheless inescap-able as parameters of choice.

There are further important implications of such a choice. The choice of presence is, ideally, an elimination of otherness (which is why no dialogue is really required by it). And so the book is to a large extent a meditation on sameness, on "immutable emotions" (Craik 1968, 8), and on feelings based on habit (Apter 1976, 209). The essence of a personality is thought to be what the individual always and unchangeably is, and possession of such a personality can mean sharing that unchanging essence. But this conception is inevitably problematic, insofar as it has to be reconciled with a sense of community, of openness to other people with other personalities. Sameness of this sort means restriction of interest as well as avoidance of change: the outsider Lockwood puts it with his usual politeness: "people in these regions," he reflects, "live more in earnest, more in themselves, and less in surface change, and frivolous external things" (102). Nelly Dean, his fellow narrator, in similar spirit, speaks approvingly of Catherine's "wondrous constancy to old attachments" (106). This is, therefore, a world of repetition. The way that the second generation of characters (Linton Heathcliff, the younger Catherine, Hareton Earnshaw) repeat the relationships of the first generation (Edgar Linton, the older Catherine, Heathcliff)—though with many differences—has often been pointed out, and the text itself does not spare in noting the persistence of situations: "It was the same room into which he had been ushered, as a guest, eighteen years before: the same moon shone through the window, and the same autumn landscape lay outside" (317). This may seem to be not far from banality, since moons and landscapes never change much; the point is in the change that actually has taken place (Heathcliff is now master, not guest) within an unchanging framework: so Heathcliff is an usurper, an inauthentic substitute for the true master Edgar Linton; the permanence of nature is paradoxically called on (through a cliché confirmed by English culture) to bear witness to the overthrow of traditional culture.

More generally, this is a book rich in substitutes, proxies, and representatives, from Hindley Earnshaw exercising power in his family as a "detestable substitute" for his dead father (62) to Linton Heathcliff and young Catherine suffering Heathcliff's power as "representatives" for his dead enemies in the Linton dynasty. *Wuthering Heights* is rich in analogies and resemblances, as well. In the passage last quoted, Heathcliff goes on to say that Hareton and Catherine are reminders of the first Catherine (so that, as far as the younger Catherine is concerned, "I heartily wish she were invisible—her presence evokes only maddening sensations")—but so too is the rest of the world, including Heathcliff's own features. The resemblance is a physical one, obviously not dependent on analysis or judgment but grapsed intuitively—and by an intuition so undiscriminating as to eliminate all individuality.

Most important, perhaps, is that this wish to possess the presence of another person is profoundly endogamous. The younger Catherine revealingly comments that "people hate their wives, sometimes, but not their sisters and brothers" (271); love is kept within the family. The example she very pertinently quotes is Heathcliff's aversion to Isabella; the strongest positive evidence of family ties is given by the connection of Heathcliff and Catherine, who have been brought up together almost as brother and sister (and Mrs. Leavis goes so far as to speculate, on rather slight evidence, that they biologically are half-brother and sister), a connection disastrously broken by Catherine's choice of an exogamous marriage to Edgar Linton and restored only in death. The completeness of this connection is made clear in a

famous speech by Catherine in which she declares that "I *am* Heathcliff" (122), which Mrs. Leavis rightly sees as an assertion of her
fidelity to her own origins in Wuthering Heights (Leavis 1969, 125).
Endogamy means identification of the self with the other, suppression of differences. The point is not without its paradoxes, like so
many points of the book, because one view of Heathcliff throughout
the novel is that he is an outsider, a gypsy-like child of unknown
origins who acquires wealth from an unknown source, a cuckoo who
supplants the rightful children. Catherine's identification with him
can only be asserted by a chain of hyperboles and metaphors, and
some of them are rather awkward: "My love for Heathcliff resembles
the eternal rocks beneath—a source of little visible delight, but necessary." There is a powerful and poetic commitment to the eternal,
marked by the superbly taut rhythm of the first half of the sentence
and the dense suggestions of "eternal"—unchanging by contrast with
the gracious foliage that represents the attractions of Edgar Linton
but also immortal, transcending humanity; but there is also a pedan-
tic, cautiously litotic and abstract explanation of the metaphor in the
rhythmically unbalanced second half. The excitement of identification (with Heathcliff and with changeless nature) is instantaneous:
communication of this excitement of the skeptical Nelly Dean takes
time and calls for self-conscious caution. Nelly Dean, in fact, un-
imaginatively dismisses this as "nonsense," while admitting that she
can make sense of it, and recalls Catherine to a moral view of marriage. The cult of sameness is shown to fit ill with social life and to
put a strain on language, which is shown as social communication
and not essentially as visionary outpouring.

The fascination the novel has so long exercised (and not least the
admiration shown for it in the French surrealist tradition, as for instance by Bataille 1957, who sees in it a mystical search to replace
dualism by an instantaneous transgression of the limits of individuality) must surely depend on this romantic aspiration to transcendent
sameness, which in a radical form would exclude language, and which
certainly does come close to excluding dialogue. But there is otherness in the novel, and there is dialogue. There are the contrasts of
the urban sophisticate and the provincial, of the unengaged or only
partly engaged observer and the actor, of refinement and roughness,
of the powerful and the powerless, of the desired and the rejected.
Each group has its own language; and much of the interest of the
novel lies in seeing what is common to these languages (in other

words, what the author thinks is inherent in any speech at all in the world she has created) and in seeing how these languages come to terms with each other. Often the speech of characters may stop short of full and equal communication. It may constitute an attempt to repress the other party's speech, as a "dialogue des sourds" (as is, to a considerable extent, Catherine's discussion with Nelly Dean about the eternal rocks, which Nelly as narrator nevertheless fully records for the interest of Lockwood and ultimately of the reader). And the end of the novel is in fact a recantation of this mystical privacy: it shows the coming together of Hareton and the young Catherine, an Earnshaw and a Linton, an uneducated man and an articulate woman, in a slow, clumsy, naive but wholly genuine dialogue. The novel passes from a power-seeking individualism that acutely fears physical separation and seeks perpetuation, in the first generation, to a timid alliance that gradually constitutes a community through the acceptance of change. This is the "destruction and re-establishment of harmony" analyzed by Lord David Cecil (Cecil 1970, 137)—though Cecil's opposition of storm and calm may seem too simple a structuring of the many contrasts and conflicts that operate in the novel—or the "reconstruction of morality" noted by Sagar (Sagar 1976, 158). The development may seem an anti-climax to some readers; the text, quite deliberately, leaves us to make our own choice as to what its ultimate vision is: is it the perpetuation of mystical passion in the walking of the ghosts, reported very plausibly a page before the end of the book, or is it the rational relegation of the story to the past (the declaration in its last sentence that the novel has really reached an end) by Lockwood, who is skeptical that "anyone could ever imagine unquiet slumbers, for the sleepers in that quiet earth"?

It follows from the wish to exclude otherness which is so central in the book that language will be distrusted, and so it is. Characters speak ironically of eloquence (pp. 290, 305). They keep silent: Heathcliff from childhood on is remarkable for his silence, but he is only an extreme form of the sparseness of utterance that largely characterizes the world of *Wuthering Heights* and that profoundly shocks Lockwood in the opening pages. Lockwood at first likes to think of himself as a misanthrope, shunning communication with his fellow beings; by the end of the novel he is castigating the inhabitants of Wuthering Heights as "clowns and misanthropes" (335). What has happened in between is, partly, that he has taken a fancy to the young Catherine, but more crucially, he has found out what misanthropy is really like. Compared with Heathcliff and his household, Lockwood is a chatterbox. Emily Brontë herself appears to have been highly reserved and uncommunicative (Gerin 1971); she seems to have attributed her own qualities to many of her characters—though without approving of them.

In the opening section, Lockwood has discovered what it is like not to be talked to, but only talked about. The sensation appears with absurd crudity when Catherine, whom he has invited to invite him to tea, instead brusquely turns to Heathcliff and asks, "Is *he* to have any?" (54). Heathcliff "savagely" replies "Get it ready, will you?", ignoring Lockwood's assumed needs. Wuthering Heights obviously is no place for tea parties. (Thrushcross Grange has not been much better on the occasion of Heathcliff's return from his mysterious self-enrichment, when Edgar, formally polite or devoted to habit, insists on tea being served as usual, but tea hardly lasts ten minutes, 136.) Tea parties, like other decorous social occasions, like occasions where sociability matters, depend on some approximation to an assumption of equality. At Wuthering Heights there can be no such assumption: the society there is dominated by the power of Heathcliff and so deprived of any sense of companionship (it is a serialized society in Sartre's terms). Talking about someone but not to them is a means of excluding them from community, of treating them only as objects of power. The example is perhaps a trivial one, though not insignificant: the rhetoric of the novel requires its themes to be approached through the essentially comic Lockwood in order to highlight the strangeness of the tragic Heathcliff, his distance from the sophisticated reader. But the reader learns that Heathcliff has met with this same treatment on a major scale throughout his childhood. When, after the death of his protector old Mr. Earnshaw, he has fallen under the brutal power of Hindley, he is deprived of speech ("degraded" is the key term: it largely means the adoption of a peasant accent and peasant inarticulacy, and will be manifest again in Heathcliff's "degradation" of Hareton) and becomes the object of speech by others. People talk about him: notably the Lintons speak about him as a person beyond the bounds of society: "'A wicked boy, at all events,' remarked the old lady, 'and quite unfit for a decent house! Did you notice his language, Linton? I'm shocked my children should have heard it'" (91). Heathcliff and his language are excluded; the Linton children are forbidden to speak to him, so that at their next meeting Edgar speaks insultingly about him, in his hearing, and is answered by having a tureen of hot apple sauce thrown at him—but he still virtuously insists that he has not infringed instructions by actually speaking to him. It ultimately is such treatment that alienates Heathcliff and drives him away from Wuthering Heights.

This eagerness to exclude certain communication continues through much of the novel. It is perhaps in this sense, at most, that one can say that "there is no public life in *Wuthering Heights*" and "no such thing as society" (Sagar 1976, 127), though one should not forget that such exclusion is itself a social act. At one period, Catherine, avoids speaking to Nelly Dean "except in the relation of a mere servant" (128); Edgar reduces to a minimum any contact with his sister Isabella after she has married Heathcliff, regarding her now merely as a member of Heathcliff's family (183) (again marriage and fraternal relations are in conflict); Heathcliff in turn loses contact with his wife and with their son until her death; young Catherine is prevented by her father from communicating with Linton Heathcliff, and then prevented by Heathcliff from communicating with her father until his final illness. Even when characters are together, their conversation often consists of a refusal to communicate: questions, for instance, are unanswered, or the answers are evasive or irrelevant. Most effective in this respect is perhaps young Catherine, and her technique is a significant one: by jeering at Hareton's accent and manner, she makes him ashamed to speak and so protects her privacy. Shame is an instrument of social authority which protects the Linton superiority and the Linton love of isolation. But Heathcliff himself can neatly exploit the same mechanism: instructing Hareton to "behave like a gentleman" and entertain Catherine "as nicely as you can," he confidently announces, "I've tied his tongue" (252). As long as Catherine and Hareton don't speak to each other, they can be intimidated by Heatcliff's recently acquired gentlemanliness; their speaking to each other means the end of the Heathcliff regime.

With the fear of communication, of contamination by moral poison (133), goes the fear of intrusion. Lockwood's visit to Wuthering Heights in the first chapter is, he feels, regarded as an unwanted intrusion; the Lintons' visits to the Heights during their youth are an infringement resented by Heathcliff; Heathcliff's return constitutes an invasion of Thrushcross Grange. Any contact conducive to change, it seems, is an objectionable intrusion. Similarly, the caution shown throughout the novel toward eavesdropping or overhearing testifies to an acute sense of privacy, though it has to be overcome if the story is to be told: Lockwood and Mrs. Dean are involuntary witnesses (70) to a lot of things without which the story would be unintelligible. It must be overcome, too, if the story is to exist at all. It is because the young Heathcliff accidentally overhears a conversation in which the older Catherine declares that she could not marry him that he leaves Wuthering Heights to enrich himself (121). The scene reveals something of Heathcliff's impatience: had he stayed a moment longer, he would have learned that Catherine loves him nevertheless. But it also is revealing of the lack of total privacy that is part of the way of life of the Heights, which is one of promiscuous presence, in which it is natural for people to sit about unobtrusively behind the furniture (unlike the more orderly and categorized life of Thrushcross Grange). It is also revealing of the inescapability of class discourse: hearing his "degradation" spoken of yet again, Heathcliff is hearing the Linton exclusiveness endorsed by the one person to whom he is most attached.

But if much of the use of language in *Wuthering Heights* attempts to inhibit communication, this is far from being the whole story. Much of the novel's language seeks, more than anything else, to establish the mere fact of communication. The point is powerfully made in the early sections of the novel, which constitutes a demonstration of various kinds of unsatisfactory speech. Lockwood first meets at Wuthering Heights silence and third-person comment: that is, insufficient communication. He is next exposed, in his dream, to excessive and one-directional communication, namely the sermon on forgiveness in four hundred and ninety-one sections (a sermon which, though its farcical presentation surely renders inappropriate the solemn treatment accorded it by Miller 1963, 187–90, does anticipate the many genuine acts of forgiveness which constitute a real strand of spontaneous human contact in the later parts of the novel). Then he is a witness, involuntarily, to an act of frustrated communication: he has a nightmare in which the child Catherine calls to be let in to the house and, telling Heathcliff of this, overhears his host in turn calling out to Catherine to come in. She doesn't, of course: her spectre "gave no sign of being" (70); her message is for the narrator Lockwood and not for the actor Heathcliff, because the essence of the novel is to be precisely this frustrated longing for contact. The calling, mutual but unanswered, makes a harrowing opening to the novel: it is foregrounded by an unprepared act of sadism in Lockwood's dream as he cuts Catherine's arm viciously on the broken window pane, and by Heathcliff's shamelessness in calling out his passionate evocation (in what may seem at least slightly sentimental terms) without making sure of Lockwood's departure. The apparent urbanity of both Lockwood and Heathcliff has been put to the test and has failed; this astonishing simulacrum of contact has led to violence and vulnerability.

This instance is an extreme one. But much of the dialogue in the novel shows a similar eagerness for contact, frequently reinforced by a sense of power or of challenge. This is what constitutes the remarkable openness of the characters to each other that has been noted (Miller 1963, 168–69). "Come, you shall take notice of me," says the young Catherine to Hareton (343); Heathcliff marks his calendar on the days the first Catherine spends with him "to show that I *do* take notice" (110). "I shall oblige you to listen," Catherine says to Nelly Dean (120); the younger Catherine wants to make Hareton talk (343); she reminds him because he "can't speak to me" (341), just as her mother has reprimanded Heathcliff because he "might be dumb" (110). Differing conceptions of companionship are at stake here: mere presence or conversational interchange (and the "silent companions" mentioned by Isabella, p. 215, are obviously no true companions, though they may be something of a guarantee for her own isolated superiority). What is common to these conceptions is the sense of being entitled to demand sociability, to exact it by willful action.

This is reflected in many of the speech-acts performed by the characters. They curse, challenge, dare, recriminate, accuse, scold, taunt, complain: all activities that suppose some personal responsibility on the part of speaker or hearer for the situation being discussed. This supposition is often a very debatable one, so that a good deal of conversation is concerned with rebutting the interlocutor's remarks on the grounds that he was not entitled to make them (in women, this tactic is called sauciness). "Don't you cant, Nelly," says the child Heathcliff (89), dismissing as inappropriate her conventional moralizing as he starts the story of his first visit to Thrushcross Grange. "You are incurable, Heathcliff," she replies at the end of it. "I'm going to be good," he tells her some time later; "High time, Heathcliff," she firmly replies.

This means that an extraordinarily high proportion of the conversations in the novel are quarrels or verge on being quarrels. This is a language that corresponds to a "permanent and unceasing attitude of aggression" (Miller 1963, 167), and it shows an appropriate range of verbal strategies: characters echo each others' words, in irony or refutation, they speak ironically or hyperbolically, they ask questions of surprising directness; names are replaced by emotive descriptions; resolutions and judgments accumulate in emphatic parallelism, often broken by the force of brusque or expansive passion that produces asymmetrical rhythms. This is a language of high energy. There is little redundancy in conversation. Characters rarely speak to approve or endorse the existing situation or the views of other characters; in *Wuthering Heights*, communication most typically is conflict.

The narrators insist quite strongly on this tendency. They describe or characterize a great many of the characters' utterances, and usually in no cautious terms: speakers growl, their manner is surly, they speak wildly, condescendingly, in a sweet, low manner, warmly, angrily, with curbed ferocity. What must be made unambiguous in the characters' utterances is the manner in which they are pronounced, because this reveals their emotional import; and by naming the emotional implications, the narrators gain some measure of comprehension of the energy that produces them and assert their right to judge them. Narrative itself thus tends to be openly polemic. Thus Nelly Dean refers to Heathcliff at one point as "the black villain" and adds, "I detested him just then" (50). The time relations are subtle. Heathcliff was a black villain "just then," as shown by his remarks which Mrs. Dean is relating. But is he still? The grammar would seem to imply that he is, but the narrative as a whole doesn't entirely confirm that view. Thus it looks almost as if the narrative act itself is being distanced, relegated back to the time narrated, so that it doesn't need to be taken literally as a communication in the present; the narrator's polemic becomes a spectacle rather than a message addressed to Lockwood or the reader.

If aggressiveness is typical of much of the speech in the novel, there also are important kinds of language which are less aggressive. They normally take the form of monologue, and sometimes of written monologue, as with Catherine's diary or Isabella's long letter to Nelly Dean. One also may recall Catherine's dream narrative, Isabella's long spoken narration to Mrs. Dean of the fight between Heathcliff and Hindley, the young Catherine's confession of her meetings with Linton Heathcliff; and a number of startling outpourings by Heathcliff: his story of his first visit to Thrushcross Grange, his long account of his relationship with Isabella after their marriage (typically described by Nelly Dean as "the talk of a madman," 188), his horrifying and pathetic confession of having inspected Catherine's dead body (a narration which in fact leads up to another account of his fight with Hindley, so that the conflicting monologues go together to give a sense of distorting mirrors), his confession of disillusion with his policy of revenge. No one also should forget that a large proportion of the text is made up of Nelly Dean's lengthy narrative monologue to Lockwood, and that the whole text comprises Lockwood's diary-like reminiscences of illness, exile, and isolation.

These narratives differ perceptibly from the practical language of interpersonal relations. They are marked—to varying degrees—by coherence in judgment, by lucidity and firmness in motivation and psychological analysis, by precision in the relation of physical action, and above all, by a beautiful delicacy in the description of natural scenes. And they differ from practical speech also in something less obviously attractive: a curious uncertainty of register. The child Heathcliff, for instance, in his account of Thrushcross Grange, refers to "a little dog shaking its paw and yelping, which, from their mutual accusations [Edgar and Isabella's], we understood they had nearly pulled in two between them" (p. 89). The first words, about the little dog, bear witness to Emily Brontë's skill in reproducing oral English, which is superbly demonstrated in many other sections of the novel. The relative clause, and especially the intercalated phrase about "their mutual accusations," has no such spoken quality. The words would be completely indefensible if judged as a plausible account of what someone might say; what they do is to show that narrative can be bookish: enjoyed for its own sake and for the spectacle it conveys and not simply used as a means of coping with the interlocutor as so much speech is used in the novel; bookish because it approximates to the detached view of the narrator, which is a comprehensive view capable, in this instance, of eluding emotional impact. In Heathcliff's direct impressions the sight of the dog and the hearing of the accusations (which moreover obviously occupy some time in a conversational sequence, here summarized in the word "mutual," which adds a further element of distance from the immediate moment of perception) are important as grounds for his deduction; but in his narrative style the deduction appears to be contingent only on the dog. Narrative, consistently with this slightly embarrassed stance of detachment, is often a matter of curiosity (112), or idle curiosity (358), or represents the view of the cool spectator (195).

Such implications demonstrate what is not always apparent in the novel as a whole: that speech is not necessarily the result of emotional engagement.

It is isolation that produces these unrestricted and expansive texts, often explicitly so. Mrs. Dean comments, with mild unease, that she tells these pathetic events by way of "amusing a stranger to the family" (288); Lockwood's character as an outsider is what makes the story conceivable. Isabella, confined in Wuthering Heights with Heathcliff and his uncouth dependents, writes, almost at random, to Nelly Dean in search of the "common sympathies of human nature" which are totally lacking there. "Humanity" may be, as Heathcliff suspects (190), a mere cant word for the Lintons, who are chiefly concerned, as we have seen, with refinement and distinctiveness; but here perhaps it has real meaning. Certainly Heathcliff himself at least recognizes an overwhelming need for community, which produces his final anguished outbursts. His long speeches are all startling, simply because of his habitual reserve; his life, even more than that of the other characters, is one of abrupt and unpredictable gestures. Often, of course, these gestures are of physical action: sudden departures, blows, embraces; but his speech partakes of the same uneven rhythm. And he makes the quality of one such sudden change very articulate: "my mind is so eternally secluded in itself, it is tempting, at last, to turn it out to another" (353).

Heathcliff has led a life of power and seclusion. He has had little intercourse with those around him, except to assert his will. This reclusion he presents in this observation not just as a seclusion of his person, like, no doubt, that of Edgar Linton in his last days (219), which is, like Heathcliff's, a sign of mourning for Catherine but also a sign of how far his house and grounds are sufficient to his needs. Heathcliff's seclusion is one of his mind. The intense mystery as to what is going on inside him, the enigmatic quality often noted in him, his refusal to exteriorize, is precisely what gives rise to the suspicion of a deep and unchanging preoccupation on his part, and therefore what makes him so intriguing to the narrators and to the reader. He offers the picture of a mind hidden from the public because, presumably, he has only two objects: his love for Catherine (and the text certainly comes very close to implying that such love cannot be talked about, cf. Miller 1963, 175; to talk about it would imply a combination of love and self-consciousness which is very difficult to maintain in terms of the framework of concepts of the novel, but which is at least approached in this final monologue of Heathcliff) and his desire for revenge against those who have humiliated him ("I never relent in exacting my due, from any one," he has told Lockwood, shortly before, p. 334, with reference to the rent he is owed, but perhaps not only to that). Now his secluded energy is to be turned outwards in speech—though still under strict safeguards: Nelly Dean is enjoined not to talk of what he tells her. She does, of course, talk about it to Lockwood. The context of Heathcliff's wish to escape seclusion is a precise, subtle, and imaginative statement of the incompatibility of his two concerns, of the way Hareton and the young Catherine have come to be transmuted in his mind from representatives of his enemies, and so objects of revenge, to representatives of himself and the older Catherine, and so objects of obsessive contemplation. It seems then as if it is impossible to maintain within oneself a mere two ideas, if those two ideas are themselves felt as contradictory.

The transformation—the conversion, one might even say—in Heathcliff's thoughts is a fundamental one. He is not relieved by his confession to Nelly Dean; the skepticism about speech evinced through so much of the novel is not finally overcome, and Heathcliff relapses into silence and mystery. No one quite knows what happens to him in his last days. But it would seem to be this: in his confession he describes Hareton as "the ghost of my immortal love, of my wild endeavours to hold my right, my degradation, my pride, my happiness, and my anguish—." Able, at last, to see his own feelings as ghostly, through the refraction of his proxy Hareton, able to stand away from them sufficiently at least to name them, Heathcliff is then enabled to see, not just the ghost of his love, but the ghost of his beloved, or at least to believe wholly that he does so. Real or imagined, the vision of Catherine's ghost is a fulfillment for him, and he has no further need to live. Speech leads to silence, illumination, and death; though it has not been a relief, it is a release.

But all this is speculative. What the reader confidently knows is what transpires through Nelly Deans's skeptical commonsense. Perhaps this is inadequate (Craik 1968, 22); but its very inadequacy is significant. We learn two things from her. The first is that she is strongly convinced that something of Heathcliff's inner life has at last been disclosed (she reminds Lockwood quite emphatically that he could have had no inkling of Heathcliff's mind when they met, though in fact Heathcliff's evocation of the dream ghost may have given him some notion of it). The second is her wish to keep to herself the nature of his end: she seeks, in vain, to close his eyes, "to extinguish, if possible, that frightful, life-like gaze of exultation, before any one else beheld it" and says nothing of his possibly suicidal refusal to eat, "fearing it might lead to trouble" (365). (The trouble it might lead to is presumably a refusal of interment in consecrated ground, and so the frustration of the final dubiously harmonious vision of the three tombstones.) Mrs. Dean, the central narrator of the novel, is a witness and, as she claims, a privileged witness both to Heathcliff's speech and to his silent deathly self-expression. That she can recount them both to Lockwood authenticates her position, so that Heathcliff, who has reduced so many other characters to possessions, becomes almost a possession of hers. Almost because the eyes will not shut: "they seemed to sneer at my attempts, and his parted lips, and sharp, white teeth sneered too!" It is the physical presence of Heathcliff, his frightening, deathly, domineering presence that has ultimate significance in the novel; and what it signifies is perhaps the body's challenge to rational talk.

Note

1. References in the text are to E. Brontë, *Wuthering Heights*, ed. D. Daiches (Harmondsworth: Penguin, 1965).

3

JANE EYRE

"—and so much annoyance she caused me daily and hourly, with her incomprehensible disposition and her sudden fits of temper, and her continual, unnatural watchings of one's movements! I declare she talked to me once like something mad, or like a friend—no child ever spoke or looked as she did."[1] The speaker is Mrs. Reed, Jane Eyre's aunt and the persecutor of her childhood, and the moment is a privileged one—one when truth is spoken—Mrs. Reed's deathbed. She is speaking to the adult Jane Eyre, though, characteristically, she does so in the third person, because during her childhood especially, but not only then, a lot is said about Jane rather than to her, and much of it is harsh and unsympathetic. Mrs. Reed's view of Jane will be disqualified, in an important sense, a few pages later, when she admits that her annoyance at Jane, and especially her resentment at the same outburst of anger on Jane's part to which she refers here, has led her to lie about Jane's fate to her relatives and so to deprive her of an inheritance. The pattern is striking: a sudden act of self-expression, disrupting Jane's persistent taciturnity, what her aunt calls her "incomprehensible disposition," and disturbing the otherwise inert and tyrannical relationship of aunt and niece, leads to the disruption of family ties and so of inheritance; but the novel restores the inheritance, carefully traces the family connections which Mrs. Reed has suppressed, and justifies Jane's anger (so proving that it is possible to be both rich and irritable, or, more generally, both part of a social continuum and subject to brusque changes of temperament). But even if the overall structure thus tends to exclude Mrs. Reed's view, it has at least been given forceful expression here, and it does correspond to a large extent with what we learn of Jane through her own narrative.

The accusation in short is that Jane is mad or fiendish. (A suggestion that she is somehow inhuman recurs throughout the book: her employer and future husband Rochester has already commented that she has "rather the look of another world" [153], and when she returns to his home, Thornfield, after Mrs. Reed's death, he will exclaim that "she comes from the other world" [272]. When, at the end of the story, she finds him in Ferndean, he feels the need to ask, "You are altogether a human being, Jane? Are you sure of that?" 462.) Silence and sudden passion are interpreted as extra-human, and these on the part of an outsider to the family, an "interloper" as Jane is more than once called, but who will nevertheless gain property within the family (Jane is an heir), who is a subject of frequent bewildered discussion—Jane is being accused of being Heathcliff. But whereas *Wuthering Heights* remains centered around the unintelligibility of the outsider, of the character who crosses the bounds of class and family, *Jane Eyre* is narrated by the outsider. Its author's task has been to capture that incomprehensibility in a first-person narrative, from inside.

The task is a challenging and important one. On the whole, telling one's own story, giving an account of oneself, is likely to be seen as automatically rendering that story intelligible, as giving at least an appearance of relating the past self to the narrating self, of justifying or explaining what one has done and thought, of making it natural. But Jane Eyre is not unambiguously natural; or at least she forces her readers to ask what naturalness means. She is alien to Mrs. Reed, who fails to find in her (and with good reason) any "sociable or child-like disposition" and calls on her for behavior which is to be "lighter, franker, and more natural, as it were" (39). She is a "strange child" even to the affectionate servant Bessie, who considers her "a little roving, solitary thing" (71). Rochester finds "something singular" in her (162). She places herself (not least through her uncompromising desire for independence) in strange and ambiguous situations: appointed as governess in a house where she starts by mistaking the housekeeper for the owner, she later combines the status of governess with that of intending mistress of the house; departing from Thornfield, she arouses suspicion through her ladylike begging; she refuses the normal womanly role of clergyman's wife offered her by her cousin St. John Rivers, and demands the nonexistent role of female curate. Jane is a person made up of paradoxes, and so she shows up the paradoxes of a society which regards a docile sociability as part of nature, which regards women as especially spiritual beings but denies them spiritual office, which makes independence synonyous with deprivation, a society in short which rejects the integrity of the personality but at the same time subjects relationships to rigorous hierarchy and conventionality. All this points to yet another layer of paradox: how can so paradoxical a character present herself through a discourse which tends toward transparency and normality?

An important part of the answer is this: the utterances of the young Jane have to be incongruous or otherwise discontinuous with their context, as it is constituted in the narrative of the older Jane; and they have to be discontinuous or incongruous with each other. Less central characters, by contrast, can be largely redundant in their utterances. Or at most they may show a steady development in what they say. Important people, such as Jane, Rochester, St. John even, are "changeful and abrupt" (158); and if minor characters have uncharacteristic speeches, as at Mrs. Reed's deathbed, then those are the crucial speeches, the ones that show up the incongruities and disharmonies of their social situation.

Jane's utterances (and those of some other characters) are made to stand out from their context, first of all, by a recurrent stress on the difficulty and uncontrollability of speech. A great many of Jane's early speeches, especially, are pronounced awkwardly or involuntarily. Asked by the kindly apothecary Mr. Lloyd what makes her unhappy, the child Jane finds it difficult to frame an answer, and then "bunglingly" complains of her cousins' and aunt's cruelty (56); she complains of her aunt's exclusion of her from the society of her own children (rather as Heathcliff is excluded from the world of the children of Thrushcross Grange) by a "scarcely voluntary demand," in which "something spoke out of me over which I had no control" (60). The outburst of anger of which Mrs. Reed complains is pronounced in a state of "ungovernable excitement" and bears witness to the "uncontrolled play" of her feelings (68–69). In getting to know Rochester, later, she relaxes to the extent that "the answer somehow slipped from my tongue before I was aware" (162), and later again, somewhat reluctant to spend too much time with him, she admits "that though my tongue is sometimes prompt enough at answer, there are times when it sadly fails me in framing an excuse" (277). Frustrated by the discovery that Rochester is already married, despite his proposal of marriage to her, an exclamation "burst involuntarily from my lips" (332). Often, speech is not a matter of will. Jane's nature is impulsive (she expects contact with Mrs. Reed to "re-excite every turbulent impulse of my nature," 70); the novel offers us not just the psychology of phrenology to which Karen Chase has so lucidly drawn attention (Chase 1984, 56–57), which tends to a static conception of a person's faculties, but also a psychology of impulses. That phrase may not seem to make sense, because it might seem that impulses, being unpredictable, do not lend themselves to any psychology. In fact these impulses do reveal something persistent and intelligible in Jane's character, namely the healthy, natural responses of a sincerely Romantic personality: anger at the Reeds' injustice, frank recognition of Mr. Rochester's ugliness (but it is a dynamic, attractive ugliness), a sense of the need for divine help in time of crisis. What is unpredictable is their timing. The concept of the impulse implies a conflict between natural sensibility and social control (and self-control); the conflict is essentially spasmodic, and perhaps the more tense for that.

Impulsiveness produces uneven rhythm of speech. This is the case not only with Jane, who varies from extreme laconicism to lengthy and highly coherent narratives such as that in which she recounts the frightening dream which culminates in her waking to see Bertha Mason, Rochester's true wife, attacking her wedding dress (308), but also of lesser characters such as her cousin Eliza, who, generally wanting no company and no conversation, "suddenly" produces a tirade of more than three hundred words, in highly articulate and rhetorical style, announcing her dislike of her sister Georgiana (264), or the servant Grace Poole, Bertha's guardian, who spends much of her time carrying mugs of porter about in silence but on one sinister occasion utters a longish "harangue" (185) opaquely warning Jane of the dangers of finding out too much. There is something under the surface, one might say, in these cases: Charlotte Brontë's insight is that what we are inclined to call a surface may be a habit of silence, and that silence is precarious.

"I know no medium," the narrating Jane says; "I never in my life have known any medium in my dealings with positive hard characters, antagonistic to my own, between absolute submission and determined revolt. I have always faithfully observed the one, up to the very moment of bursting, sometimes with volcanic vehemence, into the other" (426). These sudden and vehement outbursts make for much of the energy of the novel. The movement of the novel is to place Jane eventually in an environment in which vehemence is unnecessary because no question of submission arises: but before that time it has implied a rather uneasy admiration for her moments of intensity, which prove both lasting integrity of character and an inexplicable dividedness of character.

The division in Jane Eyre can be viewed very largely as a division between inner life and outer life (and again the movement of the novel is eventually to bypass the opposition). It takes uncomfortable and intriguing forms: sullenness, aggressiveness, a restrictive purposiveness, a provocative attentiveness, an inner theatricality.

Jane barely replies to much that is said to her, or she confines herself to monosyllabic answers; she rarely initiates conversations or new topics in conversation; if she has some specific wish for information, she interrogates people with brutal rigor, as, for instance, when she asks Helen Burns at their first meeting about her book, the school, its name, Helen's parents, the school's income, and many more things, which Helen copes with in a spirit of efficient economy (81); many of the conversations in which Jane participates (especially with Rochester) are provoked by her silently staring at her partner (as Mrs. Reed notes) or by her conspicuously strange or distressed appearance. One may note, too, that even on the occasions when Jane does voluntarily open a conversation, the point is sometimes obscured by the form of the text, which may merely paraphrase her opening remark but give in full her interlocutor's answer (e.g., p. 132, with Adele). Typically, Jane is a listener during much of her story: Rochester predicts that she will find herself "the involuntary confidante of your acquaintances' secrets," recognizing "that it is not your forte to tell of yourself" (167). She resents being known; she objects to Rochester's attempts to "draw me out—or in" (231) and is anxious when, in disguise, he reveals unexpected knowledge of her, wondering "what unseen spirit had been sitting for weeks by my heart watching its workings and taking record of every pulse" (228). On this occasion she confesses herself to be an eager narrator; and she is still less at ease when St. John Rivers insists on "converting you into a listener" (405) and telling her the whole of her own life story, which she has been attempting to conceal from him (in other words, he retells the plot of the novel so far, with amplifications): her transposition from the role of narrator to that of audience gives a sort of impersonality to the facts recounted, which both authenticates them as not being her invention, and highlights her passivity, revealing how far she is a victim and a beneficiary of circumstances independent of her desires. Listening to other people's stories is the mark of the outsider; listening to one's own story is the mark of a dependence on the network of society which conflicts with Jane's status as outsider and with her fierce individualism.

If less perversely and offensively self-effacing than Lucy Snowe in *Villette*, who, for instance, hides for a considerable period both from the reader and from Dr. John, apparently a new acquaintance in the foreign city of Villette, the fact that she has recognized him as a friend of her youth, and who if anything rather boasts of being "in public, by nature a cypher" (*V*, 324), Jane Eyre is nevertheless fundamentally uncommunicative for much of the novel. Her story begins when she isolates herself from the Reed family at Gateshead Lodge, secluded in "double retirement" in a curtained window seat with a book, which offers her romantic visions of forlorn deathliness, images which will continue to preoccupy her later in the novel. Art provides a substitute for human contact. Linder (1978 35) points out how the solitude of the artistic imagination, adumbrated here, gives a starting point to the whole development of subjectivity that forms part of Jane's significance throughout the work. If here Jane's isolation is explained by the Reeds' rejection of her as unnatural and unchildish, one cannot help noticing that she retains a distaste for contact, by inertia possibly, throughout much of her life. Even when she is addressed with concern or interest, as she often is by Bessie, for example, and even not infrequently by Mrs. Reed, her replies can be brief and uncooperative in the extreme. She forces Rochester, for instance, to require her to speak:

> "Speak," he urged.
> "What about, sir?"
> "Whatever you like. I leave both the choice of subject and the manner of treating it entirely to yourself."
> Accordingly I sat and said nothing. "If he expects me to talk for the mere sake of talking and showing off, he will find he has addressed himself to the wrong person," I thought. (164)

Characteristically, Jane's longest utterance here is a silent one, and it is a refusal of speech, based on a bleak inability to see the value of communication. Other characters, of course, do talk "for the mere sake of talking and showing off": the most obvious case is Blanche Ingram, the fashionable and ambitious young lady who is Jane's rival for Rochester's hand, and who is presented as unremittingly vulgar and crudely self-displaying (as a sort of more seductive Mrs. Elton): artificial in expression and naive in self-praise. The novelist, it is easy to think, has little imaginative sympathy with Blanche's type, and she is allowed to remain on the level of fairly crude caricature. It is certainly no overstatement to say with Martin (1966, 79) that this language is almost burlesqued, made into a sort of play-acting. This is partly, no doubt, a matter of keeping Jane in the center of the reader's attention and gaining sympathy for her. But it also is partly a matter of the novel's fascination with secrecy: because Blanche has no secrets, she has no character.

At first, Rochester himself appears to have no secrets. He tells Jane, his governess, at an astonishingly early stage of their acquaintance, of his past love affairs, and does so with an openness which she might well have been expected to find outrageous. Jane, however, regards this confidence precisely as a shared secret, as a "tribute to my discretion" (177); and she still senses another secret in him. He does, of course, have another secret, as he indicates by explicitly "talking like a sphinx" (169). The real secret is not his illegitimate affairs but his legal marriage, to the insane Bertha. It is the overcoming of secrecy that makes him a worthy partner for Jane; love has to be achieved as the culmination of a process of difficult learning. Rochester is fascinating—for Jane and for the reader—as a combination of extraordinary openness and extraordinary deceptiveness. The almost Gothic machinery of the plot, with the mysterious figure in the attic, not very carefully guarded by a taciturn or misleadingly persuasive servant; the puzzling visit of the sophisticated stranger, Richard Mason, in fact Bertha's brother, who is made victim of her sudden violence (an outburst more direct and intense than Jane's purely verbal vehemence) and with whom Jane is left, in a striking display of her master's power and secrecy, under strict instructions to hold no conversation with him at all—all this is an image of Rochester's hiding; and what he has to hide is not the spontaneous self-awareness of Jane's inner life but a natural passion corrupted, in his account, by the pressures of an artificial society. One of Jane's rivals, Blanche, the intended bride, is too obviously and publicly the voice of conventional class-based self-esteem; the other, Bertha, the established and rejected wife, is secretly and privately the voiceless manifestation of ill-directed vitality. Between the two, Jane, the successor to Bertha, is natural enough to transgress class distinctions (she is a "plebeian bride") and passive enough to minister to Rochester rather than threaten him or require his ministration. And she has enough interior life to allow change and fascination.

There is a rich vein of theatricality in the novel, much of it disapproved of, if with some ambiguity (one recalls the portrait of the actress Vashti in *Villette*, a source of fascination and disquiet). There is Brocklehurst's ostentatious preaching and his forcing of Jane to display herself as a guilty child; there is the prattle of Rochester's putative daughter Adele, with her skilled recital of verse (she's the daughter of an actress); there are the charades in which Rochester and Blanche Ingram enact a marriage. This open theatricality perhaps reaches a peak in two scenes.

One is the episode in which Rochester disguises himself as a gypsy in order to tell the fortunes of Blanche and her party, and of Jane. This episode is curious, partly because of a sort of occluded theatricality: readers don't see the gypsy Rochester with Blanche, only her disappointed and frustrated reaction. We are left with a sense that theatricality is going on, that it is effective, and that it is perversely effective: the force of the gypsy's information produces a baffled silence in Blanche (conspicuous communication, that is, inhibits normal communication). The effect grows more complex when Jane is summoned to hear her fortune in turn. The pretense, thin enough at the beginning of the scene when the gypsy, with unwonted literary learning, makes known her dislike of the "vulgar herd" (221), grows ever less serious as she speaks in Rochester's style, with his wit, his firmness and rapidity of judgment, and his persistence in questioning. Rochester is himself and, simultaneously, an assumed personality; he thus symbolizes his love of truth-telling, makes it conspicuous, dream-like, fictitious. The truth he tells, ultimately, is his physiognomic view of Jane's character: an optimistic view, in general, seeing her as made of conflicts but thinking the conflicts will be won by conscience and human affection for an interlocutor. It is a view which the novel as a whole endorses, but not one confirmed by the novel so far, by what Rochester actually knows, because Jane is still very much subject to "the eternal silence of solitude" which he wishes to see overcome. Theatrical disguise allows an open communication of a truth which has yet to be validated, and the fiction of the novel enters into complicity with this fictive prophecy.

In this scene, Rochester displays Jane to herself. In another scene he displays another woman, and without disguise. If the gypsy scene is the truth of the future, this other scene is the truth of the past.

Rochester, after his marriage has been prevented by Richard Mason and his lawyer, Briggs, displays Bertha to them, Jane, and the clergyman. "I wanted her [Jane]," he says, "just as a change after that fierce ragout. Wood and Briggs, look at the difference! Compare these clear eyes with the red balls yonder—this face with that mask— this form with that bulk; then judge me, priest of the gospel and man of the law, and remember with what judgement ye judge ye shall be judged!" (322). The essence of Rochester's gesture is an exposure of sexuality to judgment, specifically to those crucial institutions of judgment in nineteenth-century England, the church, and the law. The exposure takes the form of display and contrast (and no mild contrast, at that): desire is made a matter of blatant choice.

By contrast, Jane's theatricality exists only within herself; it takes the form of soliloquies (one of which [356] is explicitly named as such). The prevalence of the soliloquy in the presentation of her thoughts is very striking: soliloquies are much more prominent in placing (though not, of course, more frequent) than the alternative forms of psychological presentation, free indirect discourse, or summary of thought, and they are much more conspicuous in style, because the essence of a soliloquy is to contrast with the narrative context (at the very least in deixis and tense); in fact, Charlotte Brontë heightens the contrast by making it the vehicle of inner debate.

The process first appears in almost laughable form (as Eagleton remarks) with Jane's decision to leave Lowood, where she has been a teacher, to seek out independence. Independence is one of the keynotes of her character, and this situation brings out how far independence has to be economic, and how far it affects her belonging to institutions: private employment is more independent than public employment. (Later, the inheritance Jane hopes for gives her, in the phrase of the time, but used with special aptness, "ever so small an independency," 297.) Having made her decision, Jane *thinks* with all her might: "What do I want? A new place, in a new house, amongst new faces under new circumstances. I want this because it is of no use wanting anything better. How do people do to get a new place? They apply to friends, I suppose. I have no friends" (118). And so, exhaustively, it goes on, in question and answer. The lucidity is impressive: the bare contrast of the insistent desire for novelty with the recognition of helplessness, the careful apprehension of reasons and conditions of action, the steady progression from end to means. But it is naive, too, and awkward. She is being too explicit within herself, telling herself things she already knows, becoming a spectacle for herself.

The tone grows more severe, more alienating later. Reprimanding herself for her obsessive interest in Rochester, she says: "You have nothing to do with the master of Thornfield, further than to receive the salary he gives you for teaching his protégée and to be grateful for such respectful and kind treatment as, if you do your duty, you have a right to expect at his hands . . . He is not of your order: keep to your caste, and be too self-respecting to lavish the love of the whole heart, soul and strength, where such a gift is not wanted and would be despised" (192). Jane the writer is rather proud of this speech, which she carefully asserts is not meant to humble her "by a slavish notion of inferiority." But the "you" in itself indicates that the inner debate here is reaching an acute state. The speaker is hardly identifiable as the passionate natural Jane; it sounds more like a Lowood schoolteacher; this is a voice of authority, class-distinction, contractual duty, and fear of contempt. The intensity of inner life that produces this self-apostrophe and with it the strained periphrases (the master of Thornfield is Rochester, more often called "my master" or, later, "my master and lover") and the highly conventional abstract vocabulary of moral terms, as well as the more characteristic Romanticism of "heart, soul and strength"—which, however, is negated—makes up a drama of depersonalization, of repression of desire in favor of an inert reciprocity of obligations. But this, too, is going to be cancelled. The framework of moral and psychological analysis it implies will be superceded when, a few pages later, restored to the presence of Rochester and seeing him in contrast with the artificial Ingram set, Jane feels "akin" to him, believes he is, not of her "order" but of her "kind." "Did I say, a few days since, that I had nothing to do with him but to receive my salary at his hands? Did I forbid myself to think of him in any other light than as a paymaster? Blasphemy against nature!" (204). She adopts the first person; she shifts to a style of rhetorical questions and exclamations; she names her own former speech acts ("say," "forbid") and in so doing she summons up nature as an opponent to money; affinity as an alternative to class. And yet this is still a statement of suppressed and restricted emotion: "I know I must conceal my sentiments . . . I must, then, repeat continually that we are for ever sundered—and yet, while I breathe and think, I must love him" (204). Silence and continued repetition—

these are the conditions of passion in much of Charlotte Brontë (and most consistently so, perhaps, in *Villette*).

The outspoken Rochester himself is cautious when it comes to declaring his feelings for Jane, notably in the long speech in which he hypothetically asks if he would be justified in marrying her (246–47). Jane, searching in vain for "a judicious and satisfactory response," is as inarticulate as ever, and in effect refuses to recognize his proposal as such, thus driving him back to Blanche by her assertion of spiritual independence. "'Sir,' I answered, 'a wanderer's repose or a sinner's reformation should never depend on a fellow-creature'" (247). The novel as a whole refutes this view; Jane finds her repose in Rochester, and Rochester finds his reformation in Jane. But the doctrine can seriously be put forward: it is seen as part of the firmness of character and sobriety of speech that make Jane admirable, as well as part of the inhibition and diffidence that constitute her immaturity. The restraint on communication implicit in the gap between her public elusiveness and her private self-discipline is generally complementary to Rochester's conduct: he is publicly challenging (demanding information, forcing Jane to utterance) and secretly guilty. But here that restraint has spread to Rochester, too, and it will be by a devious path that his directness is restored. He does, in fact, at last propose to her directly and tenderly, in response to one of Jane's uncontrolled outbursts: "The vehemence of emotion, stirred by grief and love within me, was claiming mastery, and struggling for full sway, and asserting a right to predominate, to overcome, to live, rise and reign at last; yes—and to speak" (280). She speaks from passion; her emotion ceases to be inner drama and becomes, vehemently, an open and eloquent statement of her delight in shared talk and her resentment of social necessity. Speech here is beyond constraint and beyond convention: "it is my spirit that addresses your spirit," she tells him; "just as if both had passed through the grave, and we stood at God's feet, equal—as we are!" The Heathcliff note is powerfully there again; what it substantially amounts to here is the claim that ordeals make equality manifest. Rochester is to pass close to death, in the fire which destroys Thornfield, and Jane has previously risked death in her wandering from Thornfield to Moor House and has then undergone the more practically relevant task of refusing the appeal of St. John Rivers to accompany him in a life of evangelical endeavor. The novel endorses her rhetorical vision, her sense of a purified conversation of spirits, if only in a curious mitigated way.

The Romantic element of the novel is, as Chase very rightly stresses, much circumscribed (far more definitely so than the corresponding elements of *Wuthering Heights*); and yet it is precisely the fact that Jane can speak in terms of such hyperbolic Romance that precipitates the conclusion of the novel and Jane's own maturing. Reciprocity in *Jane Eyre* is often a principle of inflexible discipline: "It is my way," Jane comments,"—it always was my way, by instinct—ever to meet the brief with brevity, the direct with plainness" (372). But in the present instance her speech is not just an apt response (as during much of the book her speech tends to be limited to a barely adequate response): in this proposal she takes the initiative and earns a reciprocal openness from Rochester. This is no longer his mocking, shameless, aggressive openness, but an openness of spontaneous commitment. The commitment is partial; we shall find as much when the wedding service is interrupted. The hints are already there in his savage accent and look and in his oddly defiant monologue: "For the world's judgement—I wash my hands thereof. For man's opinion I defy it" (284). We know Rochester is unconventional; he has often told us so. Why does he repeat it now? In fact, this is an echo of his earlier hypothetical or speculative proposal, though it is not recognized as such, and a proof of uncertainty of social relationships. The proposal is a sign of unconventional passion—or, to put it another way, of guilty cynicism toward his true wife; and for the Christian that Jane more or less is and that Rochester is to more or less become, it is an abuse of the sacrament of marriage. And he doesn't forget the fact; but nor does he communicate it fully to his own bride. Hence a deviant speech, not a silent soliloquy like Jane's, but not a communion of spirit with spirit either.

Jane, then, most commonly, in the earlier part of her story, is outwardly disciplined to the point of refusing communication, and inwardly passionate enough to produce energetic soliloquy. But the balance can be inverted, too. Her outer expression can be one of immediate passion, and her inner life can be dominated by inhibitory abstraction. The dialectic is complex and constitutes a telling diagnosis of the crippling of emotional life by the restrictions of power, dependency, and an impersonal code of dutiful acceptance; it gives proper weight also to the power of inertia. "The Lowood constraint still clings to you somewhat," Rochester tells Jane (169). She behaves at Thornfield as she has learned to behave at Gateshead and at Lowood, and only gradually learns to act as Rochester wants her to.

(In other words, she gradually shifts from the shaping influence of Brocklehurst to the shaping influence of Rochester—an improvement because Rochester is "her kind",—and then escapes, after his failure, to become more wholly herself by resisting the shaping of St. John Rivers.)

Jane survives Lowood and outlives its influence. But there is one aspect of Lowood that, curiously, she does not fully transcend, and that is the voice of Helen Burns. Helen Burns is the first full object of Jane's love (after the kindly affection of Bessie at Gateshead); she is a model of Christian resignation to the rigors of the school. One of the early climaxes of the novel is the scene in which Jane falls asleep in the arms of Helen, who dies before they wake. The scene is harrowing in a way rather different from anything that happens later in the book; it creates an association of love and death which is not fully endorsed by the whole work. And Helen, in this last scene as throughout her life, is the vehicle of a language which seems to be taken very seriously but which contradicts the major drive of the novel. At worst this language falls into a clumsy pedantry; at best it sounds like this: "Hush, Jane! you think too much of the love of human beings; you are too impulsive, too vehement: the sovereign Hand that created your frame, and put life into it, has provided you with other resources than your feeble self, or than creatures feeble as you" (101). True, this does suggest one aspect of Jane's resolute independence, and it anticipates her consistent, if vague, piety. But it does so blandly. It denounces the vehemence and impulsiveness that make Jane fit to be the heroine of the novel; it denounces them in the name of a being too remote to be named, except as a "sovereign Hand" and, in vague circularity, as "resources," and it requires its hearer to view herself as a mere "frame" and as a "feeble self" (and Jane is surely not feeble). It is conventionally humble language, high in redundancy and remote from concrete actuality. But the adult Jane, reporting her youth, records it at some length and with apparent gratitude. At Helen's death, she feels, in silence, some reserves as to Helen's confidence in immortality: but she makes no other comment on her embracing of death, except to remark on the sweetness of her tone (113). Helen is a model of acceptance, and shows the price of acceptance, in her slightness of speech as well as in her early death. Jane is to attain maturity through resistance; but she has paid tribute here to a life which does not seek growth, a life which does not allow for change and so is incompatible with the novel (the novel

as a genre, as well as the novel *Jane Eyre*). She has shown a sort of
beauty in the lack of need. In doing so, she no doubt disquiets her
readers; but perhaps rightly so, insofar as she demonstrates that the
dissatisfaction which is at the root of the novel is not inevitable, that
it is an option in life and itself open to judgment.

Here, then, on the level of narrative, is yet another discontinuity
of Jane's language, yet another unresolved paradox. There are others.
Jane's narration is a mosaic of different manners (as Mrs. Gaskell
neatly commented on Charlotte Brontë's style in general, Gaskell
1908, 215). One symptom of this is the frequent disruption of tempo-
ral sequence by the switch to the present tense. More substantially,
there is a fine mobile impressionism, as in the first vision of Mr.
Brocklehurst: "I looked up at—a black pillar!" (63). There is an
energetic and detailed descriptive manner with a delicate shifting of
rhythm and sometimes a range of intense metaphors: "That beck
itself was then a torrent, turbid and curbless; it tore asunder the
wood, and sent a raving sound through the air, often thickened with
wild rain or whirling sleet; and for the forest on its banks, *that* showed
only ranks of skeletons" (107). There are intelligent generalizations:
"Children can feel but they cannot analyze their feelings; and if the
analysis is partially effected in thought, they know not how to express
the result of the process in words" (56). There is acute psychological
analysis as in Jane's reflections on her character at the time she is
separated from her beloved teacher Miss Temple: "I had given [?] in
allegiance to duty and order; I was quiet; I believed I was content;
to the eyes of others, usually even to my own, I appeared a disciplined and subdued character" (116). So far, these various styles
can be seen as conveying aspects of a coherent character, mature,
reflective, and observant, though they are conveyed with differing
degrees of closeness to experience and differing degrees of imaginative interpretation of the object of discourse: from the violent metaphor of "torn asunder" to the heavy insistence on textual cohesion
in "the result of the process."

But there are other sides to her, again. There is a pompous face-
tiousness in the reference, for instance, to a fellow teacher's snores
as "her habitual nasal strains" (117). There are abrupt apostrophes:
"Yes, Mrs. Reed, to you I owe some fearful pangs of mental suffering" (52). There are elaborate periphrases which muddy the point of

view: "'I should indeed like to go to school,' was the audible conclusion of my musings" (57). Above all there is the constant anxiety about the reader's expectations and the degree of his or her information: "Let the reader add, to complete the picture, refined features; a complexion, if pale, clear . . ." (80). (However, there is nothing as outrageous as the chapter opening in *The Professor:* "Reader, perhaps you never were in Belgium?") Most of the narrative of *Jane Eyre* is the work of a mature, relaxed Jane; but there is still a constrained respectable Jane as well, a narrator who needs approval and seeks it in abstraction from her experience. The open and restricted Jane can come very close together, as in this attempt, in the introductory account of Thornfield, to reconcile description and explanation: "an array of mighty old thorn trees, strong, knotty, and broad as oaks, at once explained the etymology of the mansion's designation" (131). The language in which the trees themselves are evoked is aptly energetic; the statement that their presence explains why Thornfield was so called makes desperate gestures toward learning. But it is not enough to say that the phrasing is unfortunate. The very awkwardness is significant: the phrase seeks to reconcile a private directness of sensation and feeling with a public rationality of knowledge, and its failure suggests that private and public still do not quite mesh.

On a larger scale, this same difficulty is apparent in the construction of the latter parts of the novel. Little has been said so far of what happens to Jane after her departure from Thornfield. This is because what happens is that she escapes from the problematic sense of communication to which she is prey in the early part of the novel, the view of language as exclusion, discipline, and violence, which is the starting point of *Jane Eyre*. Little by little, she takes the initiative in conversation, speaks more freely and with less rhetorical strain, and acquires the skill of eliciting speech from others (notably, she forces St. John Rivers to grant her his confidence, much as Rochester has forced Jane's own confidence). She argues, analyzes, expresses feelings; her range of syntax, rhythm, and figurative expression extends. Finding herself an equal (at least) to her companions, in family status and in fortune, no longer an outsider, satisfying her "craving for kindred," she acquires increased competence in speech. This happens gradually; as narrator, she does not comment on her development, which proceeds with an air of normality that seems to allay the disruptiveness of much of the text, until finally she makes a decision. Once she finds that this family, too, like the one she escaped from at the beginning of her story, is an establishment of authority, she rejects it. That is, she rejects the temptation of a sort of endogamy, of being part of her cousin St. John, of thinking like him: she again becomes an outsider, restored to Rochester, an outsider like herself. She "cuts the bonds of kinship" in what Eagleton regards as a bourgeois self-creating style (Eagleton 1975, 26). This happens suddenly, by an intervention of a strange sort, by a preternatural communication. Just as she is most tempted to yield to St. John, she prays to Heaven to show her the right path (444). She is "excited more than I had ever been" and the revelation that follows may be a result of that excitement—so it seems that excitement and Heavenly guidance coincide. Whereas previous excited states had made Jane prone to unpredictable self-expression, this culminating excitement makes her abnormally receptive to communications from without; she hears Rochester's voice calling to her, though he is many miles away, and calls back asking where he is. She then traces him to his second home at Ferndean, finds him ready to marry her, thanks to the death of Bertha, and learns that at the moment when she heard his voice he had actually called her name. He had, in fact, pronounced it with "frantic energy"; it "broke involuntarily from my lips," he says (471), just as Jane's earlier appeal for divine help "burst involuntarily from my lips" (332), and he has heard her reply. Spontaneous energy here disrupts the text for the last time. It inaugurates an age of stability and reconciliation and of unrestricted talk, talk which is "but a more animated and an audible thinking" (476). The paradox remains at the conclusion of the novel, then: Jane gains through domestic order and gradual change, but she can put to use the experience she gains only by something like a miracle—which is also something like her childish uncontrollability, reversed. Eagleton regards this mysterious communication, together with the general stress on the involuntary in the novel, as clumsy engineering designed to exonerate Jane from responsibility for her actions (1975, 61–62). It is more than that; it is an assertion that rational will is insufficient in an authoritarian and divisive society. Charlotte Brontë divides the self, undermining the even and self-possessed progress of Jane's narrative by disparate gestures of exceptional transforming force, not just as a novelistic convenience, but from a sense that the self cannot be unified because the stable order of public responsibility is incompatible with the unforeseeable acts of private passion.

Jane Eyre is a book dedicated to change. "Is change necessary to happiness?" a character in *Shirley* asks (*S*, 452); the answer is "yes." "Is it synonymous with it?" "I don't know." Change does not seem to be synonymous with happiness in *Jane Eyre;* but happiness does depend on the vitality of will that also produces change (which takes Jane through five places of residence, for instance, releasing her from "the fetters of a uniform and too still existence," 147). The question the book highlights, beyond that, is whether change is continuous growth or a sudden supplanting of the past, and specifically whether the voice of the young Jane, with her evasiveness and her impulsiveness, is an anticipation of the usually even, confident voice of the later Jane. The answer implied in the novel is complex and indecisive; it depends in part on the sense of personality as constituted by a constant conflict of kinds of utterance, and of resolution as being the holding of conflict in abeyance; and it depends also in part on a sense of the novel as a harnessing of rational and supra-rational, of predictable and unpredictable, in a mixture which is inescapably fictive. Hence the combination of real emotion with a fairy-tale atmosphere which is noted by Martin (1966, 80), or, in Craik's terms, "the tensions, and the resulting balance, between her natural impulse towards the thrilling and supernormal, and her firm belief in the importance of the rational and the everyday" (Craik 1968, 69). Eagleton speaks of Charlotte Brontë's novels as "'myths' which work towards a balance or fusion of blunt bourgeois rationality and flamboyant Romanticism, brash initiative and genteel cultivation, passionate rebellion and cautious conformity" (Eagleton 1975, 4). The tension so often commented on is indeed central to Charlotte Brontë's imagination. In particular, it is implicit in the central stylistic and structural principles of *Jane Eyre* as we have seen them, the principles of secrecy and suddenness, and her major originality is perhaps precisely to place these two things at the heart of the individual's personality and of interpersonal relations.

To this extent, the novel may be irresolute, but its irresolution is part of its importance. If it seems at times to give too much credence to Romantic conventions, to spontaneous goodwill, to the outsider as lucid consciousness and moral arbiter, to past guilt as a condition for future redemption, it queries all these things, too. And in so doing it queries how adequate is the conception of independent individualism and solitary self-discipline which still forms part of our range of interpretations of personality, and how far that conception is valid only in the context of a complementary conception of personality as social action.

Note

1. References in the text, unless otherwise indicated, are to C. Brontë, *Jane Eyre*, ed. Q. D. Leavis (Harmondsworth: Penguin, 1966). Other references in the text are indicated as follow: *S*, *Shirley*, ed. H. Rosengarten and M. Smith (Oxford: Clarendon Press,1979).

4

NORTH AND SOUTH

"Edith!" said Margaret gently, "Edith!"
But as Margaret half suspected, Edith had fallen asleep.

North and South begins with a failure of contact. The heroine, Margaret Hale, with her usual mildness, wishes to talk to her fashionable and beautiful cousin, who is about to contract a prosperous marriage. But Margaret is unable to, and she remains separate from the easy well-being of Southern England and peripheral to the more sophisticated and worldly members of her extended family. The novel ends with another sort of exclusion, and a less passive one. Discussing with her new fiancé, Thornton, the reaction of their relatives to the news of the engagement, she whispers, "after some time of delicious silence" shared with her beloved, "How shall I ever tell aunt Shaw?" Aunt Shaw is Edith's mother, and the voice of a crude Southern intolerance of the North, which is Thornton's home. Margaret still then feels some interest in her family, but now it is very clearly subordinated to her newfound maturity in love. Thornton replies that he can guess Mrs. Shaw's reaction:

"Her first exclamation will be 'That man!'"
"Hush!" said Margaret, "or I shall try and show you your mother's indignant tones as she says, 'That woman!'"

And so, presumably, they fall back into loving silence. The hush is attained in the course of a relaxed and frank exchange in which each rejects their families, the embodiments of the inflexibilities of North or South. The novel has passed from an uneasy dependence on family to a confident replacement of family by love, and from a frustrated or partial communication to a readily chosen intimacy of silence. The sequence is a normal and, in itself, unremarkable one; it is the sequence of growing up. In *North and South* this process has been

75

made the subject of a long and difficult evolution, in the course of which the novelist has reflected closely on the relation of individual to society, on the conditions of social and personal harmony, and on the ethics of speech and silence. The result is a work in which many of the concerns of the nineteenth-century novel—duty and freedom, secrecy and publicity, shame and responsibility—are given cautious and complex consideration. It has been well said that in Mrs. Gaskell's eyes, the family is a "stifling and often blighting influence in children's lives" (Lansbury 1975, 8); *North and South* is a story of how the influence can be overcome, and a demonstration of how persisting and diffuse it can be.

A crucial moment in this evolution of the heroine occurs when she hears Thornton, still comparatively unknown to her, discussing industrial relations with her father, Mr. Hale, a Southern clergyman who has abandoned his living after feeling doubts and has moved to the Northern town of Milton to make a living as a tutor. Thornton, a hard laissez-faire economist of the Manchester school, speaks dismissively of his workers, expects conflict between masters and men, and feels no obligation to explain to the workers the economic problems which he believes condition his strategy and which he explains coherently enough to his equals, Mr. Hale and Margaret. Margaret, who has been making the acquaintance of a working-class family in Milton, and who has learned something of the hardships of working-class life, wishes to see cooperation and communication between employers and workers (a wish which the novel itself clearly ultimately endorses, though gradually and cautiously). She doesn't quite communicate her wish to Thornton. He comments:

> "We, the owners of capital, have a right to choose what we will do with it."
> "A human right," said Margaret, very low.
> "I beg your pardon, I did not hear what you said."
> "I would rather not repeat it," said she; "it related to a feeling which I do not think you would share." (164)[1]

The softness of speech is there again; it goes with an indirectness and economy of conversation which suggest that this discretion of speech is not just consideration for the partner in dialogue, but a wish to muffle and avoid contact (she is forced to spell out in her next speech that she recognizes the human right but regards it as secondary to religious principle, a context barely hinted at in this first fragmentary utterance). Most crucially, she declines to complete her remark, on the grounds that it "relate[s] to a feeling which I do not think you would share." Speech relates to feeling; so much the author unmistakeably would endorse. But what Margaret implies is what she has to learn to surpass in the course of the novel: the expectation that feelings are simply given, that each individual has his or her own feelings which need not be exposed to public discussion, and that no speech is worthwhile where feelings are not already shared. Her view of language is an inert one; it is that communion can only take place between people who are already alike. If this were true, no maturing would be possible, and no differences could ever be reconciled; North and South would be inescapably separate. That they can be brought together—with difficulty, against obstacles of chance and prejudice, in defiance of the norms that restrict intercourse between people of different origins and inclinations—is what Mrs. Gaskell sets out to show in the novel.

The development of this same conversation will go a long way toward showing it. Thornton takes Margaret's opposition seriously. He speaks to her "in a subdued voice, as if to her alone," and "eagerly," though later "in an offended tone": the feelings that matter to him are obviously those provoked by Margaret's judgment of him. She remains cold; she does not wish "to be so exclusively addressed," or, as she puts it, with characteristic defensiveness, she is "not fond of being catechised." She resists dialogue; she resists personal commitment in conversation, which Thornton so readily offers (so she is "displeased at the personal character Mr. Thornton affixed to what she had said"). However, she cannot resist entirely. She is persuaded to express her Christian scruples about Manchester economics, and she expresses her alienation from the conflictual society of the north. She also reveals something of her relationship with the weaver Nicholas Higgins, and at length she speaks quite eloquently of her vision of a coherent society: "The most proudly independent man depends on those around him for their insensible influence on his character—his life" (169). There is a debate going on within all this. Margaret has found society dominated by hostility ("I never lived in a place before where there were two sets of people always running each other down," she rather naively—and certainly very innocently—admits). She reacts to this by recommending a sense of dependence to Thornton. But she does so while still attempting to maintain her own independence of him and of Milton society and while clinging to her Southern isolation. Her words do not fully correspond with her conduct, and the relation of words to conduct is to be one of the main concerns of the book: feelings are the essential mediators between conduct and speech (though Mrs. Gaskell does not abandon the awareness, shown elsewhere, that "words are poor and tardy interpreters of feelings to those who love one another," Gaskell 1908, 229), and Margaret's feelings here are still unformed. On the one hand, she is drawn to her inert sense of self-defensive independence; on the other, she is unsettled by Thornton's probing and by the need to defend her judgment.

In short, then, she is to pass from family to marriage and from isolation to dialogue; the catalyst is the experience of the North, of an alien but open society. Elizabeth Gaskell shows with the balance of sympathy and judgment that is so characteristic of her, with the "rational sanity of judgment" that McVeagh has praised (McVeagh 1970, 2), the attractions and demerits of isolation, and the harshness as well as the productiveness of the challenge of the North. Her overall sense seems to be that Margaret is interesting and admirable not because of what she at first is, or even of what she finally becomes, but because she changes. The novel contains much about the unchangingness of life, in North and South alike. People complain of "longing for a bit of a change," of "get[ting] tired of sameness and work for ever" (185). They suffer, in illness, from a "monotonous life" in which there is not even any "variety of light and shade" (306). Margaret is warned by Higgins of the dullness of working-class life, which is like "soaking in stagnant waters" (382). The theme reaches a culmination when Margaret, toward the end of the novel, meditates in an eloquent and pathetic soliloquy on the "sense of change, of individual nothingness, of perplexity and disappointment" that overpowers her after she has lost her father and been separated from Thornton and Milton. She even grows aware of the potential dishonesty of her religious convictions, which may be a disguise for a wish for inertia: "I seek heavenly steadfastness in earthly monotony." But waking in the morning, she sees things afresh (not, then, significantly through thought, because the effectiveness of thought is quite clearly delimited in this novel, but through uncontrolled experience):

"After all it is right," said she, hearing the voices of children at play while she was dressing. "If the world stood still, it would retrograde and become corrupt, if that is not Irish [paradoxical]. Looking out of myself, and my own painful sense of change, the progress of all around me is right and necessary." (488)

Soon after she will recognize that "I too change perpetually" (489). She is not so distinct from the world outside her; she shares the need for change; and change, Mrs. Gaskell shows us, means interchange and the dialectic exposure to others in conflict and difference. Gilmour's view of her is concise and accurate: she is "a novelist of change, in whose finest work the social and the personal are subtly interrelated" (Gilmour 1986, 56). The North is valuable to Margaret precisely because it is a place of disputes and distrust, because it is not the South.

But even in the South at the beginning of the novel, Margaret has been something of an outsider as Craik very rightly stresses (Craik 1975, 93–94). The South produces refinement, it is true (and refinement, one can never forget in reading *North and South*, is one of the great values of Victorian England, especially though not exlusively of middle-class England, and is largely a matter of a discipline in signs and communications); but it produces it by exclusion. The world in which Margaret lives at first is a banal one, dominated by thoughts of success, money, comfort, and self-display; it is a world in which not much can be said that is original. Mrs. Gaskell shows a discreet comic sense for the triviality of fashionable conversation and for its ability to reveal: "She will be quite envious when she hears of Edith having Indian shawls. What kinds are they? Delhi? with the lovely little borders?" (37). The North is not all that much better: Margaret, with intelligent wit, complains to her father of the dullness of after-dinner conversation at Mr. Thornton's house: "It reminded me of our old game of having each so many nouns to introduce into a sentence . . . Why, they took nouns that were signs of things which gave evidence of wealth,—housekeepers, under-gardeners, extent of glass, valuable lace, diamonds, and all such things; and each one formed the speech so as to bring them all in, in the prettiest accidental manner possible" (221).

In the North, these things are opposed to the men's business of industry and profit; in the South, they are complemented chiefly by family loyalties, but these seem thin enough in their effects, as appears from the letters especially which Margaret gets from her relatives. The coarse good humor and superficiality of an unreflective

family feeling is as apparent in the letters of her brother Frederick—
for whose sake she has lost something of her reputation and her
integrity—as in those of the thoughtless Edith. In fact, for Margaret
and her immediate family, it is precisely these family links that create
an atmosphere of restraint and tense consideration for others' feelings. Frederick has been involved in a mutiny in the navy as a junior
officer and has taken refuge in exile in Spain. It cannot be said that
he suffers very much, because in Spain he marries and prospers in
the sherry trade, for which he seems to have much affinity. But he
does suffer transiently when he returns to England on the occasion
of his mother's death. The situation is an acute manifestation of the
secrecy with which he is surrounded: he even is required to sob
quietly, so he will not be heard by suspicious neighbors (316). But
even before this climactic presence, his name has been an object of
constraint and embarrassment. His mutiny is "buried in sad oblivion"
(52); eventually Margaret emboldens herself to ask her mother about
it, "if it does not give you too much pain to speak about it" (151);
her father on a later occasion leaves the room during a conversation
because "he can't bear to hear Fred spoken of" (262). Family love
(little as it may be merited: Frederick's letters about the mutiny,
misread by his mother, leave the reader little doubt of his guilt and
immaturity) is close to pain, and produces silence.

Frederick, then, is one occasion for delicacy and difficulty of communication in the Hale family. The other principal one is Mr. Hale's
doubts. These are kept silent until Mr. Hale has come to a conclusion. He then theatrically signals that something is wrong: "after tea,
Mr. Hale got up, and stood with his elbow on the chimney piece,
leaning his head on his hand, musing over something, and from time
to time sighing deeply" (65); then he communicates to his daughter
his decision to abandon his living (though still not the exact reason
for his inability to accept the discipline of the Church of England: it
may be that Mrs. Gaskell did not wish to confuse her novel by extraneous theological issues, or it may be that she wished to present a
father who does not relish discussion with his daughter). He does
not inform his wife; that is left to Margaret, in one of many instances
in the book of message carrying, of indirect communication, and she
has to do it with the greatest of circumspection. "I am a poor coward,
after all," Mr. Hale says, "I cannot bear to give pain." But she must
be told; and so Margaret has to do it, apologetically: "Dear, darling
mama! we were so afraid of giving you pain," she confesses. Commu-

nication is likely to be pain, for Mrs. Hale at least, once it touches on the real concerns of her male relatives, whether it be rebellion against the church or against the state. She lives by masking issues from herself; and it is no surprise that she fails utterly to adapt to the life of Milton, where issues are nakedly apparent; reluctant to move in at all, she dies not long after her arrival. But she is none the less loved and respected, if not quite uncritically, by her daughter and husband: her gentility is not simply rejected in the novel, as is the egoistic gentility of Mrs. Gibson in *Wives and Daughters*, but is a factor in the refinement and delicacy of the family, of the sense it holds that telling people things calls for self-discipline and imagination.

The effect of all this in Margaret herself is far from comfortable. She clings to a sort of immaturity: she has an eloquent and sincere proposal of marriage from Henry Lennox, Edith's future brother-in-law, a character who throughout the novel forms a temptation for her in that he closely resembles her ("he liked and disliked pretty nearly the same things that she did," 40). He offers no essential challenge to her, makes no demand of change; he is a sort of extension of her own brother, whom he undertakes to defend through his legal skills when the issue of his guilt in the mutiny arises. The temptation he offers is the temptation of endogamy, but even this proposal shocks her: she is ashamed to have received it, "guilty and ashamed of having grown so much into a woman as to be thought of in marriage" (65).

It is Frederick himself who involves her most deeply in real guilt. Returning home at the death of his mother, he risks arrest; he is identified by a police spy, whom he accidentally pushes off a railway platform in a scuffle while escaping. Being an inveterate drinker (as one might no doubt expect of a police spy), his injuries are complicated by alcoholism, and he dies. This causes a lot of difficulty between Margaret and Thornton, who is jealous at her being seen secretly accompanying an unknown young man; secrecy, that is, in this novel is a result of family attachments and incompatible with love. Still more seriously, it brings her into trouble with the law and with her own conscience; asked to make a statement to the police about the death of the spy, she firmly declares that she was not at the station at the crucial time. Family affection leads to lying. The police inspector who takes her statement reports it to the appropriate magistrate, who is in fact Thornton again, and he decides to hush up the matter, considering it one of his "faithful acts of service of which she should never know" (352). Guilt is spreading, and the relations of the as yet unacknowledged lovers are growing more occluded, more false.

Margaret's motives are not condemned definitively by the novel. A friend speaks of "the strong, instinctive motive" (485) which she might have redeemed herself by explaining to Thornton, and strong instincts seem to be endorsed by the author. But she is nonetheless aware that this instinct, the clinging to family and to the "natural language of expression, so intelligible to those of the same blood" (311) is something lesser than the contact of strangers who have to learn to communicate with each other in a way less directly natural but more fulfilling, and that it can be a major obstacle to such enriching contact. Family secrets lead to loss of personal assuredness; interfamily contact leads to personal growth.

But Margaret's being has always resided a little outside the confines of the family, or at least in a detached view of it. As her father cuts himself off from his family and takes refuge in learning, as he cuts himself off from his church and makes himself a "schismatic outcast" (76), as he finds himself most fully in his conversations with Thornton so that Margaret judges that it is the opposition of character between the two men that explains the attraction they obviously feel for each other (122), so Margaret has been at her best in alliance with her father, or in solitude and soliloquy, in self-discipline and self-awareness. A sympathetic and sensitive example (almost Jamesian in tone) is the presentation, through free indirect discourse, of her reflections on the Shaws' nursery in which she has been brought up for some years (so that she is an outsider in her parents' home as well as in Milton): "she remembered the dark, dim look of the London nursery, presided over by an austere and ceremonious nurse, who was terribly particular about clean hands and torn frocks" (38). Hers is, more than anyone else's, the consciousness through which the events of the novel are perceived (if the point of view shifts to that of Thornton or the police inspector, it is often so that we can see Margaret herself); she is well qualified to show us her world, because she sees it from outside, as we do, and with precision and unresting judgment.

It is in Milton, however, that she becomes most consciously an outsider; and the presentation of Milton in the book is such that it shows how far the strangeness and the tragic gravity of the place actually complement her own seriousness and vulnerability. She is never able to forget that she is a "foreigner" in Milton, as the mill-hand Higgins tells her twice (113, 183), and therefore, as he makes clear, both naturally ignorant of the town's ways and entitled to some measure of tolerance (Milton's welcome is ambiguous at best). She is exposed to the dialect of Milton, which is depicted with great plausibility by the author, and undoubtedly, with great accuracy. (Her respect for dialect is shown in her frequent references to her serious attempts to learn dialect forms from her husband, especially for the Northumberland novel *Sylvia's Lovers*; her use of dialect is often spoken of sympathetically by critics, e.g., Craik 1975, 39; McVeagh 1970, 84; Wright 1965, 258.) The dialect is a sign of difference, not of inferiority (nor I think, of superiority, as Lansbury 1975, 47, thinks; though Lansbury's view is plausible and stimulating): it is capable of eloquence, as in the striking weaver Boucher's denunciation of the Union (206); of tragic sobriety, as with Higgins' lament for the death of his daughter (283); or of telling vividness, as in Higgins' comment on Thornton's state of depression in a difficult state of trade: "I reckon I know who'd ha' been sorry for to see our measter sitting so like a piece of gray calico!" (513). Mrs. Gaskell's first novel, *Mary Barton*, is an extremely impressive demonstration (especially in view of its early date) of the possibility of telling a serious story about working people in the words of their own dialect; *North and South* is a worthy successor. (One may a little regret that Thornton is allowed to comment that his workmen "have such a sense of humour, and such a racy mode of expression!", 446; but Thornton is never distinguished by tact or sensitivity toward the working class.) With the dialect of the North go the registers connected with northern trade and their specialized vocabulary: the "hands," the "knobsticks," the "unparliamentary smoke." Margaret's relatives are horrified at her knowledge of all these domains of language, from her mother's distaste for her use of "factory slang" (301) to Edith's sneer that being able to "sound his h's" is "not a common Darkshire accomplishment" (521). Margaret is steadfast in her opposition to this form of pseudo-refinement: if her own refinement prevents her from engaging in certain dialogue, it doesn't prevent her from using the proper language for what she has to say: "And if I live in a factory town, I must use factory slang when I want it," she says (302); in language at least she is part of Milton.

More fundamentally, perhaps, Milton challenges Margaret's sense of decorum. Brought up in a world where one may not say too much or say it too loudly, she is taken aback by the openness of comment on the streets of the manufacturing town. The theme recurs: her dislike of "insolent words spoken about herself" (241) is a lasting aspect of her character, and is even approved by the Gorgonlike Mrs. Thornton, who approves little else, but "like[s] to see a girl fly out at the notion of being talked about" (395). For all that, people in Milton are talked about to their faces. Servant girls, interviewed by Margaret for a job, answer back with "unconcealed curiosity" (109). (This reverses Margaret's usual liking for one-way communication, which is met most fully perhaps by the deathly passivity of Higgins' daughter Bessy, who at one point, "leant back, and shut her eyes, and crossed her hands over her breast, lying at perfect rest, as if to receive all the ideas Margaret could suggest", 144. Margaret herself is more than once characterized as a good listener, but it never goes this far with her.) Factory workers rush along, "with bold, fearless faces, and loud laughs and jests, particularly aimed at all those who appeared to be above them in rank or station" (110). Margaret, frightened and offended at first, gradually comes to accept this brashness, and it is in this way that she meets Higgins, who encouragingly comments on her "bonny face," and with whom she at first establishes a sense of "silent recognition" (110); it is in her meeting with Higgins that "North and South has both met and made kind of friends in this big smoky place" (122). She defeats her reserve gradually, but this process will prove to be crucial in her coming to know the town and with it its prime representative, her future lover Thornton.

Milton is a place of multiple languages and full intercourse, which can be antagonistic intercourse. It demonstrates its democratic nature when it allows a weaver, though drunk and impious, to speak to a clergyman; when a maid expresses views on her employers; when Thornton confesses "simply," as Margaret recognizes with respect (128), the humbleness of his origins. It permits a multiple array of languages: the voice of Revelations, much read by Bessy Higgins, balances the grim self-righteousness of Mrs. Thornton, the forthrightness and learning of her son, the lucid outspokenness of the poor, the Oxonian wit and playfulness of Mr. Bell (Mr. Hale's university friend, but himself a Milton man, and ultimately responsible for Margaret's definitive acceptance into Milton as an owner of property there).

This multiplicity of expression calls for frequent concentration on interpretation and explanation. Words have "implied meaning" (442;

but the point also is made about the South, 58); a struggle is required to show how Chevy Chase can be relevant to cog wheels in conversation (122). People have to explain to what they apply certain words (192), or comment that "I don't quite understand his application of the word" (217; the notable word here is "gentleman," opposed in an important conversation properly emphasized by Gilmour to the concept of the "true man," 1981, 86). The conversation is developed later (253): the least one can say is that the characters have a strong sense of the relativity of social values and of the interdependence between those values and language. Characters may deliberately give "answers that were like riddles" (364); or they may feel it "a duty he owed to himself to explain, as truly as he could, what he did mean" (125). In either case, what matters is the urgency of contact and the provocativeness of speech rather than any ready comprehension. Communication in Milton is a matter of energy, and energy means difficulty and opposition (so Thornton is respected by the unionist Higgins: he is "a man worth fighting wi'", 184). It means, particularly in the case of Thornton, the exercise of will—though in his case to control speech, rather than to form it. When he finds himself about to show the depth of his feeling for Margaret, he resolves that "he could not speak in the haste of his hot passion; he would weigh each word. He would; and his will was triumphant. He stopped in mid career" (252). The rhythm is emphatic enough; it brings out forcefully how far the opposition of South and North, of the impassioned Thornton and the reserved Margaret, stimulates will, and how valuable that exercise of will is. The union of Margaret and Thornton has rightly been seen as a union of gentility and commerce (Pollard 1965, 118), or of old culture and new energy (Wright 1965, 1409); but one certainly has to recognize that it is the new energy, the North's claim to the future (Wright 1965, 138) that most arouses the author's admiration.

Margaret does not fall easily into this society. She is subject to the distrust of Mrs. Thornton, in particular, and for a long time she is separated from Thornton himself, partly because of differences in the norms of communication. The point is simply and persistently made in the theme of the handshake. A normal Northern courtesy, its absence from Southern manners makes Margaret seem hostile or scornful to him at first (128). She is far from being so, and regrets her unfamiliarity with this "frank familiar custom of the place"; but he is not to know that. There is incomplete communication between them, then, because the code of communication is not fully shared. Later—and this time presumably knowingly—after their heated discussion of industrial relations, she again fails to offer her hand, and Thornton "set it down to pride" (171). A few pages later, she wrings her doctor's hand sufficiently to cause him discomfort (174). Invited to dinner with Thornton, she shakes hands with him for the first time (214), an act of which she is less conscious than he is; she is finding her way into the Milton culture. Later she goes so far as to offer her hand after a quarrel with Thornton (much of their intercourse before their engagement consists of quarrels), and he rejects it (255). The gesture this time is really significant: he truly intends a breach of politeness, as later he shows real bad manners toward her during his time of jealousy: this is "not the bad manners of ignorance: it was the wilful bad manners arising from deep offence" (303). In both instances, Thornton intentionally makes his feelings apparent; he communicates genuinely, at the cost of refinement or convention.

Margaret is gradually won over to this openness of expression. Her inherent spontaneity of feeling gradually overcomes her code of restraint; she starts to speak freely and without inhibition. In the South she had already felt frustration at being discouraged by Lennox when she "would have liked to talk to you of what I was very full of at the time" (60): in the North it can still be said of her that "it was unusual with Margaret to obtrude her one subject of conversation on others" (302), but she does obtrude, in her anxiety to maintain communication with Thornton. She is growing impulsive, and the novel clearly approves of the change.

The outstanding demonstration of her new impulsiveness, in fact, is strikingly public. In a highly theatrical and superbly paced climactic scene, she confronts a crowd of unruly strikers, reproves their threatened violence, and interposes her body between them and their enemy Thornton (234). It is a crucial moment; she faints after she is struck by a stone thrown by a demonstrator, and as she lies helpless Thornton first declares his love for her ("inarticulately," 236, just as the crowd itself was earlier manifest as a "noise, inarticulate as that of a troop of animals," 233. Public passion does not make for precise communication, but it makes for unmistakeable communication.) This, then, is the turning point of the novel. By showing herself with a man, "hugging him before all the people" (239), she has made her strength of feeling too apparent. In Mrs. Thornton's words, she has "compromised yourself . . . and exposed yourself to the comments of servants and workpeople" (394). She herself feels shame, as she had felt it when Lennox proposed, "a deep sense of shame that she should thus be the object of universal regard" (249). Her reserve and refinement are lost.

But they are lost again, in a more complex way, and she is more seriously compromised when she is seen with Frederick. The two events parallel each other very closely: she publicly defends Thornton from lawlessness, at the cost of scandal, as she later privately defends her brother from the law, at the cost of misunderstanding. The balance of private and public, and family and love, are carefully established; and so is the greater nobility and the greater potential for personal and moral development offered by love and public. It is precisely this contrast that strikes Mr. Thornton himself and intensifies and exacerbates his feelings by making him jealous: "He shared with the mob, in her desire of averting bloodshed from them; but this man, this hidden lover, shared with nobody; he had looks, words, hand-cleavings, lies, concealment, all to himself" (387). It is a challenge to him to wrest her from this unknown person into his own possession. He has challenged her in many ways; one way she challenges him is in the vestiges of her family conspiracy.

Much of the thought of the novel is concerned with the gap between public, generalized, and class-based perceptions and forms of conduct, on the one hand, and the private life of immediate personal contact and sympathy on the other. The point is most forcefully put by Higgins, who, as a trade-unionist, is obliged to think in class terms and to sacrifice such unreliable members of his class as Boucher; as a plough goes over a daisy in the pathetic poem he quotes, so the movement of class struggle must go over the individual. When Boucher is brought to suicide, Higgins feels the pathos, as the reader does; but the novel holds that pathos in careful tension with the facts of class belonging. The author's final message is perhaps Thornton's view that the classes should seek intercourse as persons: "such intercourse is the very breath of life" (525). A modern reader may find the aspiration unhelpful or facile, given the disproportion between the casual good humor of the manager dining in the workmen's canteen and the real hardships that have been implied throughout the novel. But this is part of something in Mrs. Gaskell that does still convince: the conviction that the breath of life lies in effort to make contact with those who differ from ourselves.

Margaret, in effect, had passed from the temptation of endogamy to the acceptance of exogamy (because with Mrs. Gaskell's strong sense of the importance of inertia and gradualness in human affairs, it will be only at the very end of the novel that the transformation is complete). It is made the object of a lucid meditation in which Margaret compares Mr. Thornton and Henry Lennox, now that each has declared his love for her: Thornton's impact is far more effective: he has "mastered her inner will," even though—or because—"their intercourse had been one continued series of opposition" (256–57). Milton is a place of opposition and dialogue; it is Thornton, the voice of immediate opposition and dialogue, who is able to bring Margaret to the recognition of love through the force of his will. It appears that love, like communication, is a matter of energy.

And yet, for all Thornton's willfulness and Margaret's spontaneous emotion, they are brought together finally not by their own choice; their increasing eagerness for communication and intimacy is not sufficient to overcome the misunderstandings that have come between them. There must be an intermediary. As Margaret has acted this role between her father and her mother, as Mrs. Thornton has falsely purported to be an intermediary between her son and Margaret (393), so it appears for a while that Mr. Bell, the scholar who replaces Mr. Hale in many respects but is perhaps between placed than he would have been to make contact with Milton, may make peace between the lovers by telling Thornton the truth of Margaret's involvement with Frederick's secret. But he dies too soon, and his place is taken, with true Northern democracy, by the workman Higgins; it is he who tells his master Thornton (who has employed him thanks to Margaret's intervention) of Frederick's visit and Margaret's "keeping it close" (514). Communication, finally, is social; it cannot be confined to the couple, and love depends on a whole society, with its relations of work as well as the relations of intimacy. Margaret starts as the outsider; but the essence of outsiderhood is that it makes for a richer integration.

Note

References in the text are to E. Gaskell, *North and South*, ed. D. Collin (Harmondsworth: Penguin, 1970).

5

BARCHESTER TOWERS

The world of *Barchester Towers* is in many ways one of ideal communication. It is a world of openness, where people's utterances clearly
and fully express their personality, and in which a social harmony is
apparent in the ease and the decorum of speech. These are among
the things that make for comedy in the novel and ensure that no
threat to the community can be major or irredeemable. Unlike many
novels of the nineteenth century, *Barchester Towers* does not depend
on secrets, or, very much, on shame, and the slightness of its plot
reflects the fact. This feature is characteristic of much of Trollope;
he admits, for instance, in his autobiography, that the plot of *Orley
Farm* largely comes to an end halfway through when Lady Mason
confesses her guilt. But this does not much reduce the author's liking
for *Orley Farm;* his stress on character as the essential interest of the
novels means that he is able to appreciate the force of decision and
the complexity of relationships that arise in a state of openness, of
unimpaired communication. Much the same may be said of many
other of his works, as with the almost perfunctory mystery of *The
Last Chronicle.* As a novelist, Trollope largely lacks the experience of
the city and of unpredictable social mobility which for many Victorian
novelists means that social life is a mystery, that the people one
meets are constituted by an unknown past; he is largely concerned
with the small town and the established institution, in which each
individual is more or less known and plays a somewhat recognizable role.

Although there is no mystery, there is variety, and variety can
mean friction. The institutions of Trollope's world—the church, the
family, Parliament—are places of competition, and competition involves partisanship and suspicion and loyalty to one's own kind, and
loyalty is expressed often through a facile disapproval of what is
different or challenging (which is not to say that Trollope the novelist

refuses social challenges: only that he has a liking for characters who cling to the ordinary). The crucial question that then arises is how far the codes of the institution are in fact shared between the competing groups, how far the interest of a party can be defended by appeal to an impartial ethos. Variety in speech—between opponents and between companions, too—therefore, becomes a sign of the parameters of conflict and of its strategies. For Trollope, language is at once a revelation of the disposition of the speaker and a weapon in acquiring or resisting power; it is the essential link between the inner self and the public act; and the distance between the two is less great than in many writers of the period.

Certainly the gentlemanly church of *Barchester Towers*, with Trollope's unmistakeable approval, has a strong sense of the need to organize variety. (The major problem of the novel is perhaps that the church is not exclusively gentlemanly.) Communication is expected to be decorous, restrained, and orderly: "religion," says the saintly Mr. Harding, protesting firmly but temperately against a too enthusiastic sermon, "is at any rate not less susceptible of urbane and courteous conduct among men than any other study which men may take up" (60).[1] Urbanity and courtesy are values central to Trollope's thought (some of his most powerful novels, such as *The Last Chronicle*, *He knew he was right*, or *Is he Popenjoy?* are studies of characters who intrigue him because they do not have these values). In Mr. Harding they are tempered by a Christian or old-world meekness; they are most clearly apparent in Mr. Arabin, a man of wit and reason (168), of eloquence, lucidity, and consideration in his conversations, a man who knows when seriousness is appropriate. But even less clearly admirable characters such as the choleric Archdeacon Grantly show a due sense of what belongs to an occasion: the point is elegantly made when he refrains from expressing his disgust at the excessive liberalism and spinelessness of the new bishop, Dr. Proudie, until the very moment when he enters the cathedral close and leaves the orbit of the bishop (36). Even his major opponent Mr. Slope, the bishop's ambitious and tasteless chaplain, knows how to recognize "a subject which was probably too serious for drawing-room conversation" (55). The narrator, too, is a constant reminder of a sense of appropriacy and restraint; he explicitly refrains from transcribing some offensive term used by the archdeacon about Mrs. Proudie (37) (so the narrator is more of a gentleman than Dr. Grantly, though he at least runs the risk here of provoking in his readers the indecorous curiosity as to what the term might have been.) More seriously, the narrator reflects carefully on the propriety of writing about the clergy at all, and especially of representing a sermon in the pages of a novel: "it would not be becoming," he reflects—and the choice of term is significant , because "becomingness" stops well short of either religious awe or satirical venom—"were I to travesty a sermon, or even to repeat the language of it in the pages of a novel" (43). He does report the content of the sermon, and with a clear indication of its polemic and excessive character; but because he does not report its language (and instead uses indirect speech and summary), he avoids too open a manifestation of personality in the religious domain. The degree of skepticism that he may show—not to the doctrines of the Church but to the motives of its members—is a matter of caution for Trollope, and here the caution is itself made a sign of one of the major concerns of the novel, of respect for the separateness of certain areas of experience, and so of certain types of discourse.

With this concern for separateness and distinction goes a concern for rank. The bishop, archdeacon, and curate, each has his place, and the place decides his role in conversation. People are very frequently addressed by their title (even by their spouses), and the degree of respect with which they are addressed is carefully measured by rank. The sense extends beyond the clerical context, most conspicuously in the sports day at Ullathorne, where Miss Thorne, who is organizing the event on her land, decides to allocate different parts of the grounds to the gentry and to the general population of the area, while excluding outsiders completely. The discrimination leads to some entertaining difficulties, as the climbing Lookalofts aspire to the wrong section of the grounds; but it calls forth a certain amused sympathy from Trollope and an important statement of principle from his narrator: "It is in such definitions that the whole difficulty of society consists" (331). The difficulty of society—which arises from its changing character—is what makes it interesting; Trollope looks neither for a stagnant hierarchy nor for an undiscriminating democracy.

But he does show, for all that, some liking for undiscriminating democracy, for the removal of distinctions, propriety, and definitions, for the spirit incarnated in the dilettante Bertie Stanhope, who is undiscriminating in religion to the point of having passed through various faiths at considerable speed, and who treats everyone with equal cheer, so that he, in one of the funniest scenes of the book, can address the bishop with the good-humored boast that "I was a Jew once myself" (91). Bertie totally lacks rank; his sister, the signora Vesey Neroni, who is married to an Italian of uncertain status, has a false rank and claims to be a countess. These are outsiders, cosmo-politans; the society of England is alien to their confusions and will eventually expel them (cf. Knoepflmacher 1971, xiv, 12; Kincaid 1977, 94–99).

But as much of the life and incident of the novel arises from the social confusions of the Stanhope family, so much of its development arises from the arrival in Barchester of a group of people who are lacking in a full sense of discrimination concerning communication, who conspicuously lack, as Pollard stresses, the decorum possessed even by the archdeacon (Pollard 1978, 58). These are the new bishop, Dr. Proudie, his wife, and his auxiliary Mr. Slope. We have already seen Mr. Harding's opposition to the sermon preached by Mr. Slope, in which he takes advantage of the opportunity to denounce the ethos of the cathedral in the edifice itself, an act distasteful as a sign of enmity to the old Barchester but all the more so because of its mis-placed occasion; the Slope-Proudie party is given, in what is no doubt thought of by the author as true evangelical style, to using social occasions for ecclesiastical business and to adopting a tone which disregards rank. Therefore, Mr. Harding believes that Mrs. Proudie, who has asked the archdeacon and his associates about the progress of Sunday schools in the diocese, is interrogating and lecturing him (35), and both the narrator and the archdeacon say she has cross-examined him (35, 39). Mr. Harding, further upset by a disapproving reference on the part of Mrs. Proudie to "Sabbath travelling," prom-ises her he will preach a sermon on the subject, if she comes to his church on a Sunday (36). Religious discourse, for the more sympa-thetic characters, has its place and must be kept in it. The implication is an important one; it is that religious discourse out of place is an act of aggression.

Aggressiveness is the major dynamic and the major threat of Trol-lope's psychology in this novel (and largely so in many of his others); the vision that misplaced speech can be a weapon is a perceptive one and contributes to a defense of the sure order which reestablishes itself at the end of the story. Elsewhere misplaced language can be a tactic for ensuring a reluctantly granted contact, and one which falsifies the nature of that contact. Mr. Slope's numerous letters give clear evidence of the fact: Mr. Harding finds the tone of one letter displeasing (95) because, although its only purpose is to fix a business meeting, Mr. Slope signs himself as "your assured friend"—and Mr. Harding replies with a curt purposiveness that perhaps verges on brutality, but is no doubt to be seen as self-defense; excess communication is a contamination or a hold given to the enemy. A letter in which Slope communicates to Mr. Harding's daughter, Eleanor Bold, some information about her father's prospects is much commented on because he strays beyond the official domain to compliment her (admittedly in a quite sickening style) on her son ("my darling little friend") and her hair ("those beautiful long silken tresses") (240). Occasions become pretexts for familiarity; the defensive view of the Harding party is that occasions should not extend beyond their original function. Intercourse, on such a view, would be extremely limited; relationships could hardly develop. Contact with the new would be excluded.

There is in Barchester a widespread sense of exclusiveness in communication. So it is that the chapter at the cathedral can seriously debate whether Mr. Slope should not be completely prevented from preaching there (though some measure of tolerance prevails, 50). So it is also that the formation and preservation of parties or cliques is a central movement of the novel, neatly encapsulated in the moment when the bishop, by a "slight motion of his thumb," enlists Mr. Slope's connivence against his own wife, who is in the next room and can hear their conversation but not see their gestures. So it is, more crucially because this creates one of the major delaying factors in the relationship of Eleanor and Arabin, that any attempt on her part to defend Mr. Slope or to welcome his apparent concern for her father's welfare is read as a sign of romantic interest in him. Speech-acts can only be seen, it appears, as signifying adherence to a party; an act which in fact has an impartial sense is unintelligible in this polarized society. Many of the characters, then, have a certain coarseness in speech; the only readily acceptable meanings are those of support or hostility; and part of the interest of the novel—and one way it is not restricted to the comic conception that is its basic ground—is in its depiction of some characters who can communicate precisely and sensitively, though with inevitable difficulty, despite the partisan language that surrounds them.

Barchester is fearful of contact; Mr. Slope is an unworthy correspondent for Eleanor (262) because even the receipt or transmission of letters is thought of as an act of intercourse and so of collaboration.

Much of the novel's energy goes into delimiting areas of influence, defining domains: Eleanor's rather constrained movements between the dangerously exposed world of Barchester itself and the haven of Plumstead and the archdeacon's rectory (e.g., 153) and the frequent arguments as to whether Mrs. Proudie may or may not be in a room during a particular conversation are indications of the constant concern that contact is power and vulnerability, and therefore, that it is something to be striven for and prized. Trollope's sense of "social tactics," of the hold people may get over others, has long been commented on (*Spectator* 1983, 32); what is striking for us is how anxiety on this score can stultify so much social intercourse.

A master of the exploitation of contact is Mr. Slope, with his constant presence and his skill at finding what concerns the people who may be useful to him (Sunday schools, Mr. Harding's future, the nomination of a warden to Hiram's Hospital); he associates it with mastery of a certain rhetoric, of a clerical well-meaningness and gravity that serves to disguise self-interest as the interest of the hearer. Thus he tells Eleanor with blatant sincerity about his own candidness (absurd for the reader, to whom the confession is absolutely superfluous): "I must be candid with you as the only means of avoiding ultimate consequences which would be most injurious to Mr Harding. I fear there is a feeling, I will not even call it a prejudice, with regard to myself in Barchester, which is not in my favour" (133). Ingratiating himself with the bishop in an attempt to gain his support in a bid to become dean, he tells him: "I know your lordship so well (and I hope you know me well enough to have the same feelings) that I am satisfied that my being in that position would add materially to your own comfort, and enable you to extend the sphere of your useful influence" (300). The elaboration of syntax, with the measured pace produced by parentheses, self-correction, and supporting evidence; the concern for the other's point of view; the cautiously understated and abstract vocabulary; the ostentatious awareness of the process of communication and of the degree of certainty that can be claimed for his speech are admirable things, on the face of it: all show rationality and consideration for others. However, they are false; we see it from the very excessiveness of the precautions and from the over-insistent rhythm, a manner that tends to the monologue (at most allowing intervals for the interlocutor to agree), and the persistent awareness of selfhood and purpose: real helpfulness, we recognize, is more spontaneous. So the rhetoric, the apparent organization of speech in the interests of lucidity and of bearing witness to moral values, is actually an assertion of presence, and of a dominating presence.

Furthermore, such speech is built into a chain of authority. In the speeches we have noted, Mr. Slope claims the authority of decency and sympathy; more frequently, of course, he claims the authority of faith or of the Anglican institution. The point is made very explicitly by the narrator, who comments that the New Testament is of comparatively little interest to him, "for from it he can draw no fresh authority for that dominion which he loves to exercise over at least a seventh part of man's allotted time here below" (25). Such a reliance on authority is marked in much of his speech, from his frequent assurances that the instructions he gives are *"by the bishop's desire"* (239) or that "the bishop is desirous" that they should be carried out (100), to his easy reliance on Biblical phraseology in inapt contexts, as in his ill-advised proposal to Eleanor: "Ah! Eleanor, will it not be sweet, with the Lord's assistance, to travel hand in hand through this mortal valley which His mercies will make pleasant to us, till hereafter we shall dwell together at the foot of His throne?" (384). Mr. Slope passes himself off in what might now be called an inauthentic gesture, as a mere instrument; Trollope shows clearly enough that no one can only be an instrument. The point is made with equal clarity in the opening scene of the novel: the archdeacon, eager to be appointed bishop at the death of his father, the former bishop, hastily writes a telegram to the prime minister, who holds the right to nominate, giving news of the death—and he forces Harding to sign it. Harding agrees, with much reluctance, but turns back as he is on his way to the telegraph office to tell Dr. Grantly that the government has fallen, and that Grantly's chances of appointment are therefore lost. Again, personality is dissembled under false authority: if Harding were the authority of the telegram, it might only be a piece of information; for Grantly, the real authority, it is a call for favor. Mr. Harding, the narrator reminds us in the last sentence of the book, is "a good man without guile" (499); but guile is a major feature of communication in the novel as a whole. Because it is generally quite transparent guile, readers can enjoy an easy understanding of character and a confidence in judgment which may give the impression of a beautifully innocent fictional world, or at least of a charmingly trivial one; but things may not seem as enjoyable to the characters.

If these aspects of language show a more or less conscious exploitation of ambiguities in language function—as personal strategy or as institutional routine—(and one of the most interesting insights of Trollope is apparent in the suggestion that the deviousness of Mr. Slope is not incompatible with a certain sincerity), there is a more general obstacle to communication, which makes questions of sincerity barely applicable. That is the fact that characters have their own styles and vocabularies, their own expectations about the appropriacy of utterance, to such an extent as to make intellectual and emotional contact barely conceivable much of the time. The characters, Polhemus acutely observes (Polhemus 1982, 95), like the community, may be made up of incongruous voices. If dialogue within the characters in *Barchester Towers* is not often foregrounded, the jarring dialogue of the community is the very stuff of the novel.

If there are few secrets in Trollope, there are many misunderstandings. These may arise from the better feelings of characters: notably there is Eleanor's discretion in not revealing to her family the content of Mr. Slope's letter. Any privacy is likely to be suspect. But even when people do speak fully and with ease, there are serious gaps in comprehension. These are met, largely, with astonishment or puzzlement rather than gloom; but the implication that language might not suffice for communion is an important one, which gives strength and potential sobriety to much of Trollope's humor.

"Remember there are two ways of telling a story," Mrs. Proudie remarks (143), ways which allow for quite different views of what has happened in it (and the reader at times may have a sense of a Slope way of telling the story that is suppressed in Trollope's telling of it, the story of an energetic and principled young clergyman, who seeks to stir up the inertia and superficiality of a provincial city, only to meet with tragic defeat). The two ways may be drawn to the reader's attention by specific comment, as when the narrator remarks on the evangelical preference for the word "Sabbath" as opposed to Sunday: "Sunday, however, is a word that never pollutes his mouth" (24). So, too, we have the fine spectacle of the same content being conveyed in two ways within a single conversational exchange:

> "Is she always like this?" said the signora.
> "Yes—always—madam," said Mrs Proudie, returning; "always equally averse to impropriety of conduct of every description." (94)

The signora points to observed experience of what the bishop's wife is like, trusting to her hearer's judgment; Mrs. Proudie prefers full and polemic statement.

The arbitrariness implicit here is shown up delicately in one of Trollope's favorite techniques in the depiction of speech, the use of a very rapid and unsignalled free indirect discourse. Commenting on the signora's affectation of having on her calling card a coronet to which she is not clearly entitled, the narrator remarks: "A coronet, however, was a pretty ornament, and if it could solace a poor cripple to have such on her card, who would begrudge it to her?" (68).

The manner is very characteristic of Trollope and handled with much skill—a skill that produces a certain elusiveness. Who is it who feels that a coronet is a pretty ornament (and not a sign of serious rank) and that the signora is a poor cripple (and not a witty and competent young woman)? Hardly the narrator, of course; he is much too knowing for that. Not quite the signora either, though, for even if we know fairly little of her at this stage of the novel, it will not be long till we find out that she has much more energy of mind and purpose than this phrasing suggests. What we really know at the moment is that this is a possible view of the signora, and one that we are to associate with her own sensibility in some way: the hint, ultimately, is that this is a view of herself that she wishes to have people hold, a disarming and superficial view that masks her dangerous and disturbing qualities. But if we stop short of that hint, which we are not yet in a position to confirm, what we get is the recognition that views of character are variable, uncertain, and dependent on the language in which they can be formulated.

A clearer irony can be attached to such elusive quotations: Mr. Slope's survey of the *"carte du pays,"* in military terminology, before his arrival in Barchester (42) suggests a cynicism in conscious polemics, and guides the reader to see him as an aggressive disturber of the Barchester peace. But what of the narrator's very frequent use of mock epic terminology, often rapidly deflated: "Then up rose Dr Grantly; and having thus collected the scattered wisdom of his associates, spoke forth with words of deep authority. When I say up rose the archdeacon, I speak of the inner man, which then sprang up to more immediate action, for the doctor had, bodily, been standing all along with his back to the dean's empty fire-grate, and the tails of his frock-coat supported over his two arms" (51). Who is it who, for all the indolent comfort of the scene, wants to see the conflict of High and Low Church as a Homeric battle, with the simple heroism and the historical moment that attach to such a weighty tradition? Is it Dr. Grantly? Is it, briefly, the narrator? Is it expected to be the reader, indulging an absurd taste for conflict and sobriety? None of these, specifically, of course: Trollope's point is that people involved in conflict are likely to take themselves seriously, and that our culture, the classical culture of the educated English of his time, gives a vehicle for expressing such seriousness—and in its incongruity, it amounts to a means of insulating it, of keeping it in its place, as something not quite felt by anyone.

The use of language can be a manifestation of seriousness and commitment, but these factors vary with style and register. The novel gives a rich display of varieties of utterance: Bertie's complacent chatter, his slang and his artistic phrasing, Mrs. Proudie's severity and precision, the dialect of the farmers and laborers at the sports, the pompous gravity of the newspaper editorials, the elaboration and indirectness of Slope's letter writing (simply contrasted with the brusque effectiveness of Tom Towers' letter to him). Many phrases are delightful and memorable because they so perfectly exemplify the strangeness of a register: Mrs. Proudie's "Unhand it, sir!" when Bertie has caused her dress to be torn (85); the signora's purported view of her child, "the last of the Neros," as "the last bud of a wondrous tree" (87); Mrs. Quiverful's view of Mrs. Proudie, in true housewifely style, as being "stiff and hard and proud as pie-crust" (411). Clashes of register often make up the comic spectacle of the novel: Mr. Arabin speaking about sermons while the archdeacon talks of guano (209); Mr. Slope, fresh from his failure with Eleanor, trying to ingratiate himself with a visiting academic by talk of "so many young persons enjoying themselves so thoroughly," while the bishop, more attuned to the bureaucratic spirit of the true academic, carries on with his remarks about "the hebdomadal board" (387).

The effect of such failures of contact, as are implicit in all this, is to produce a strangely static sort of conversation. Dr. Grantly in particular is much given to repeating himself and also to repeating his interlocutor's words: the device is a fairly simple piece of characterization on the author's part, but it also contributes to a sense of oddness of language, of language being put to uninformative ends. So we get dialogues like this:

> "I can't say I felt myself much disposed to like him."
> "Like him!" again shouted the doctor, and the assenting ravens again

cawed an echo; "of course, you don't like him: it's not a question of liking. But what are we to do with him?"

"Do with him?" asked Mr. Harding. (38)

And so they go on, for some time, saying very little, indignantly on one side, patiently on the other, and with little to bind the indignation to the patience. A similar incomprehension meets Bertie Stanhope in his attempt to propose to Eleanor, in his turn:

"I am determined in this matter to be guided wholly by you."

"Wholly by me?" said Eleanor, astonished at, and not quite liking, his altered manner.

"Wholly by you," said Bertie. (403)

Proposals, like most dynamic speech, are seen as aggressive: they are met with blank resistance. Given the absurdity of Bertie Stanhope, the reader is not much worried at this point; but this general tendency does mean that Trollope has set himself an awkward task to cope with when he comes to the betrothal of Eleanor and Mr. Arabin.

More broadly, the figure of Mr. Arabin is an anomalous one in the novel; he is the benevolent intruder. His newness is explicitly commented on as an attraction for Eleanor: "And now she found to her surprise, and not without a certain pleasurable excitement, that this newcomer among them spoke in a manner very different from that to which she was accustomed" (185). Novelty on the whole is not pleasurable for the characters in *Barchester Towers* (though it certainly is for the readers of the novel; it is change that makes for comedy, as Knoepflmacher points out, 1971, 48). But Arabin is an exception, because he shows willingness to talk about things, to justify his opinions, which contrasts with the crude redundancy of much of Dr. Grantly's speech, and even with the mild self-defensiveness of Eleanor's father, and corresponds to the more liberal and questioning attitude that Eleanor has found in her first husband, the radical John Bold. Eleanor represents a position not unlike that of the narrator in the novel; she belongs to the traditional ecclesiastical society, but she is dissatisfied at the unquestioned inertia that rules it and seeks a justified inertia, which she finds in Arabin (the position, further, is not unlike the "advanced conservative liberalism" that Trollope defended in the political domain and confirms—partially at least— Gilmour's view of Barchester as "a place threatened by, yet *coping with* change," Gilmour 1986, 117). The resolution of the love interest of the novel comes close to being endogamous, Arabin being a friend and protégé of Mr. Harding and Dr. Grantly (in particular, the smoothness with which he is introduced to his parish by the archdeacon is clearly contrasted with the abrasiveness of Slope's installation in Barchester); but Trollope is eager to avoid unqualified endogamy. The relationship of Eleanor and Arabin does not run smoothly, because he shares the suspiciousness and possessiveness of the Grantly circle; communication between them is impeded not by his being a newcomer, but by his being too close to the old-established leadership of Barchester and liable to its partisan spirit.

The misunderstandings are overcome, though, and in a way that has great significance for Trollope's view of how genuine communication can evolve. Arabin comes to visit Eleanor, still in a state of indecision, and conversation is difficult (462). He utters "a few commonplace remarks about the beauty of the weather" and Eleanor replies in like manner on what the narrator very explicitly calls "the dreadfully trite topic he had chosen"; and for some time they clumsily discuss matters of no major interest to either, except for a few sincerely but perhaps incongruously revealing remarks made by Arabin. They fall silent, and then Arabin, after much hesitation, finds the determination to apologize for his previous incomprehension of her. His tone is firm, abstract, restrained, and Eleanor recognizes as much, with acute disappointment. She is impeded in replying because she starts to cry: "she had never felt herself so much at a loss for words" (464). But she does forgive him; and then the two stand for a minute, she still crying, he holding her hand, in silence: "Why did he not speak to her?" the narrator asks: "could it be that he looked for her to make the first sign?" He addresses her first as "Mrs Bold" and then as "Eleanor" (the detail recalls the less successful and more articulate proposal of the unwelcome intruder Slope, whose first major mistake is to address Eleanor by her Christian name)—and then they embrace. That constitutes the engagement: "She had been told that her yea must be yea, or her nay, nay: but she was called on for neither the one nor the other" (466). As so often in novels of this period, it is a spontaneous nonverbal communication that really matters and is both admirable and effective; the "instinctive sensitive morality" of Trollope's best characters (Kincaid 1977, 260) lies in silence and impulsiveness.

Three special points may be made about the presentation of this in Trollope. First, there is the very delicate and restrained comedy of the incongruous way this intimate conversation arises from the most banal phatic communion, in a series of quite disparate steps, as if fundamental transitions in people's relations happen by chance, the deepest aspirations being almost unrelated to or incommensurable with the social surface (unlike the conduct of many of the less sympathetic and more broadly comic figures, whose absurdity lies in the total coherence of all their behavior around some quite superficial image of themselves, as representatives of rightousness, agents of power, victims of aggression; niceness in Trollope is not far from unconsciousness). Second, there is the slightly ridiculous occasion, placed under the aegis of Miss Thorne, the likeable but unrealistic devotee of Old England with whom Eleanor is staying, who is hoping to arrange a match between her and Arabin (so that the chapter is entitled "Miss Thorne shows her talent at match-making") and to whom Eleanor immediately—and astonishingly—reports the change in her status. Again there is a contrast with Slope's proposal, which takes place at Miss Thorne's sports day (under the influence of Miss Thorne's champagne)—and with Bertie Stanhope's non-proposal. Marriage is a matter of private intensity and authenticity of feeling; but it also is a social arrangement, which is convenient or inconvenient to third parties, which sorts out the position of an unplaced widow, which neatly arranges the loyalties of parish priest. In Trollope's world, public and private need to be kept in their right places—the private must be preserved from the impingement of the public, so that we must respect Mr. Harding's "horror of being made the subject of public talk" (*W*, 78). But, if all goes well as it does in this comic work, private and public also complement each other harmoniously.

Third, one of the curiously moving confidences of Mr. Arabin in the earlier part of the conversation is that "it is the bane of my life that on important subjects I acquire no fixed opinion" (463). The phrase testifies to his usual high intelligence; it echoes his wish for "a certain rule" in religion (285). Lacking decision means lacking purposiveness; in one important subject, that of marriage, Arabin is still without fixed opinion, and the author compares him favorably with others for this reason: unlike Slope and Stanhope, "gentlemen generally propose without any absolutely defined determination as to their doing so" (462); Dr. Arabin is exceptionally gentlemanly and so, perhaps, exceptionally purposeless.

The true communication, then, is unpredictable, unplanned, and yet appropriate to a social function; in these ways Arabin's proposal is no doubt a model of what communication should be—even though it conflicts, in a graciously absurd spectacle, with the lucidity, orderliness, and unpretentious self-revelation of much of the speech in the book. But there also are two other models in the novel, and they complicate and ironize somewhat the author's admiration for Arabin.

One is the Signora Vesey Neroni, and to a lesser extent her brother Bertie Stanhope. Outrageous in their egoism as they are, they provoke Barchester to self-knowledge and articulacy. Theatrical, unrestrained, mocking, ironic, excessively truthful, eager to provoke and play upon feeling, they offer a spectacle of personal revelation without social discipline or purpose; they display an aesthetic life that resembles gentlemanliness in a caricatural way, but is none the less a source of entertainment and delight for the reader. The role of the Stanhopes in the novel is much discussed by critics (e.g., O'Connor 1983, 92; Knox 1983, 99); if they appear to some to be an extraneity, it is precisely because their freedom captures the imagination of their author and of the reader rather more than the sense of decorum, which pervades most of the novel, would seem to allow. Trollope admits the value of irresponsibility, through these characters; and the admission is a serious challenge to the sobriety of the admired figures of the novel.

The other major model of communication in the novel is the narrator. A highly dramatized narrator (as Kincaid points out, seeing in him Trollope's "most serious and pressing claim to be recognized as a major artist," 1977, 32), who recalls his own knowledge of the Barchester stalls and his own meeting with Mr. Slope, who openly expresses his own attitudes to the characters and to the doctrines or feelings they express, he is no mere representation of the author or of the business of storytelling. He also is not quite the kind of person who appears as a character in the novel. He is learned in ancient and modern literature, ready to discourse at length on general questions, and able to do so with moderation, caution, and common sense. He passes promptly from an interior view of the characters to the impingement on them of the outside world, is clear in irony and in judgment, writes what he elsewhere calls "good broad English" (*F*, 119), is dominant in his sense of what is pertinent (so that much of what the characters say is suppressed, presumably as irrelevant, by the process of indirect speech or of summary, sometimes fairly extreme, leaving only what the narrator thinks worth recalling. The narrator is the voice of a worldly, practical, kindly but unceasingly judgmental vision: to the unsteady searching of Eleanor and Arabin and the glorious self-display of the Stanhopes, he is added another authority, the authority of a flexible and humane bystander. Is the narrator less intelligent than the reader may be, or less than the dialogue often is, as Polhemus suggests (1982, 100)? The question hardly seems pertinent: at this level what matters is not choice or exclusion, but the comfortable multiplicity that makes up the course of the novel.

Note

1. References in the text are to A. Trollope, *Barchester Towers*, ed. R. Gilmour (Harmondsworth: Penguin, 1983), and (indicated by *W*) to *The Warden* (London: Dent [Everyman], 1969); (indicated by *F*), *Framley Parsonage* (London: Dent [Everyman], 1973).

6

THE WOMAN IN WHITE

The Woman in White is the story of a drawing teacher who gets the better of a count and a baronet. He gains possession of the baronet's wife, and he protects her half-sister from the designs of the count (designs inspired both by a scheming love of power and money and by an open and shameless eroticism). The count is foreign and the baronet is illegitimate, but these facts only reinforce the democratic impulse of the book: professional skill and sexual purity overcome noble birth, because the birth isn't really all that noble. The aristocratic myth of continuity, of the inherent relation of the landowner to an unchanging rural community, has collapsed in the mid-nineteenth century. Aristocrats are now outsiders, as is nearly everyone else. If Wilkie Collins pays rather reluctant tribute to a peasant society that really does not change and that regards the death of the villainous nobleman as no more than matter for gossip and indifference, his main stress throughout the novel is on the uprootedness of modern society.

It is most clearly apparent, of course, in the professional classes for whom the novelist largely speaks: the drawing teacher, Walter Hartright, begins the novel by celebrating his abandonment of his London pupils to take up an appointment at Limmeridge House in Cumberland, teaching privately Laura Fairlie and her half-sister Marion Halcombe. Disappointed at Laura's engagement to Sir Perceval Glyde, he is shipped off to Central America by Miss Halcombe's agency. He returns in time to rescue Laura from the wiles of Sir Perceval and his friend Count Fosco and settles down with her in the East End of London, to find himself, after his final triumph, marrying Laura and, after some incidental displacements, establishing himself at Limmeridge itself, as the father to its heir. Walter lives by his artistic skill; skill is a commodity and it can be sold anywhere. This is normal enough for professionals. It also applies, for instance, to

Walter's friend Pesca, who lives as a teacher of Italian in London; less markedly to Mr. Gilmore, the solicitor whose business leads him to move between London and Limmeridge and who is driven by ill health to move to Germany; and to Mrs. Michelson, the clergyman's widow, who is reduced to keeping house for Sir Perceval at his country home, Blackwater Park.

This mobility extends more surprisingly to rural England proper: in Welmingham, the village near Blackwater which holds the key to Sir Perceval's guilty secret, the parish clerk is proud of his London connections, while his predecessor Mr. Catherick was a complete outsider to the village, and so was his wife, the mother of Anne Catherick, the woman in white of the title. Mrs. Catherick's journeys between Blackwater and Limmeridge and Anne's movements between these places and London, where she is at one time confined in an asylum, constitute a major component of the starting situation of the book. (A minor sign of the sense of spatial disruption in the novel is the treatment of local dialects, presented as a source of incomprehension and pastronizing aloofness.) Novels, as we have seen in previous chapters, often show a fixed society being disturbed by strangers—by a Frank Churchill, a Heathcliff, a Slope; what is special about Wilkie Collins is that, in this novel and in many others, he shows a world which has no fixed society, a world where people are thrown together, where they are linked not by custom and common knowledge, but by contingent enterprises. This anticipates the world of the modern thriller. The commoditized world in which an art teacher can penetrate the whole of society is to become the world in which the intelligence and pertinacity of a Philip Marlowe are commodities that enable him to survey the peaks of a commercial society. However, the tension is greater in Collins. Walter Hartright still respects tradition and order, even if he sees little of them. The tension relates to a broader ambivalence in the structure of the novel as regards concepts of stability and change: Is action (and especially the activity of communication) an innovative and transforming skill, or is it the manifestation of an established design?

The instability of life in *The Woman in White* has more than one function. It ensures that no one, except ultimately the evil actor Fosco and the virtuous narrator Walter, has complete knowledge of the events and circumstances of the plot, thus creating narrative tension and an air of puzzlement, frustration, and insecurity. It creates an alternating rhythm of activity and absence (notably on the part of

Walter Hartright, whose departure for America makes possible the plot against Laura) and so demonstrates the limits of control in a novel where the sense of control is very important. It reveals the vulnerability of British society to the impingement of the foreign. Most importantly, it reflects a situation in which one of the mainstays of Victorian society and of the Victorian novel (including this novel in particular) is brought into doubt: that is the concept of legitimate inheritance. Fathers do not know their children; fatherhood is secretive and illicit.

This, in fact, is what is symbolized in the figure of the woman in white herself and in the imbroglio of which she is the victim. Anne Catherick is really the daughter of Mrs. Catherick and of Philip Fairlie, Laura's father; for this reason she bears a close resemblance to Laura, for whom she is substitued in the plot of Sir Perceval and Count Fosco. For the same reason, it is no doubt implied, she grows strongly attached to Laura and her mother, in whose honor she always chooses to wear white. The point is made with powerfully suppressed pathos through a letter from Mrs. Fairlie to her husband, in which she describes Anne with tender concern (86).[1] She does not, of course, know of the relationship, and it is assumed that Philip Fairlie himself probably did not recognize the implications of the letter (575). Hidden fatherhood produces a false and alienated communication; it inhibits intimacy between man and wife as it does between father and child.

But there is more than this. The plot in which Anne is exploited is itself designed to preserve Sir Perceval's secret, which concerns his own parentage. His father, Sir Felix, has never married his mother, and so he is not the true heir of his estates. Sir Felix, a person of unattractive appearance and foreign connections, has led a life of strict retirement. Perceval was born and brought up abroad, and has little connection with England except for his friendship with Philip Fairlie. His father's life is a "private" one (551), a life cut off from church and tenants. As Frederick Fairlie, Laura's uncle, has avoided the annoyance of society by retreating into a Poe-like world of aesthetic inactivity, so Sir Felix Glyde has avoided the annoyance of society by abandoning his public responsibilities.

This is a world, then, in which privacy, property, and hidden guilt are prevalent. Mrs. Catherick is an extreme but not an atypical example. Devoting her life to concealing the illegitimate conception of her daughter, her greatest pride is that her respectability is publicly recognized: "*The clergyman bows to me*" (507). The attack on respectability is a common theme of Wilkie Collins, and one he shares with his friend Dickens: the significant point he makes here is that it involves a restriction of community, a delimitation of each individual's sphere. "This appears to be your affair," Mrs. Catherick says to Walter—of her own daughter's death. "You are interested in my affairs. I am not interested in yours" (506). Actually, the novel shows that Anne's death is everybody's business, but this is barely recognized by the characters. Walter's interest is reproved by Mrs. Catherick as "curiosity," impinging on her "private affairs" (549), and she later insists with regard to his interest in Anne's parentage, "On this side of the grave, Mr. Hartright, whatever may happen on the other, *that* curiosity will never be satisfied" (559). The context is important: in this same letter she recounts how she has incautiously spoken to Sir Perceval of his secret and noticed her daughter "looking eagerly and curiously" at her (556), a curiosity that has led to Anne's incarceration and finally to her doom. Curiosity leads to suppression, within the world of the novel. But the novel as a genre arouses and satisfies curiosity; Anne's death can be seen as a sacrifice that does, after all, enable Walter to satisfy his curiosity, to find out the truth of biological connection within a situation of social separation, and so finally to restore the value of inheritance by establishing the child of a legitimate and loving marriage as the heir to Limmeridge.

The hostility to curiosity is most marked in Mrs. Catherick, a woman who lives primarily for her façade. But it goes with a general sense of respect for distance between people, for incomplete information, for strictly channeled communication, which affects even the sympathetic characters and which the reader may perceive as an image of a discreet and disciplined society. Growing to realize the mutual attraction between Laura and himself as they first get to know each other, Walter comments, "I shrank then—I shrank still—from invading the innermost sanctuary of her heart and laying it open to others as I have laid open my own" (90). Collins's reluctance to lay open to his readers the feelings of a major character leaves a strange gap in the book. Laura is suppressed, almost as Anne is; she speaks little, at first because of the restraint necessary between herself and Walter, she being a lady and engaged, later because she is reduced to childishness by her harrowing experiences, and generally perhaps because Walter is reluctant to communicate to us his intimacies with her. He does communicate his conversations with Marion, her half-sister and protector; these are not intimate because they have a content, which is Laura ("the one subject of interest between us is Laura once more," Marion comments, 579). In this context, of the novel's care to respect the privacy of the intimate life, one recalls one of the fine shocking transgressions it contains. Fosco gains access to Marion Halcombe's diary and, after reading it, writes his own comments in it. The comments are deeply appreciative; but the sense of intrusion, of violation, is extraordinarily strong.

More generally, there is a strict morality as to what may be communicated. When Anne writes to warn Laura against marrying Sir Perceval, she is told by Walter that "it was wrong to send such a letter" (126). More positively, people assure one another that they have "a claim to hear" (62), a right to disclose (150), a "right to ask" (178), a "right to know" (186), but they admit to having "no right to offer an opinion" (188). These rights and claims often are based on love or trust, but sometimes only on social hierarchy. They form part of a pattern of obligations which affect the use of language. Speech can impose responsibilities: people demand promises; Marion can say that "You oblige me to grant your request, Sir Perceval, when I would much rather refuse it" (156); Mr. Gilmore, coping with the indolent and recalcitrant Frederick Fairlie, comments that "my tone and manner left him no alternative but to comply with my request" (181). Speech in *The Woman in White* is almost exclusively functional (though not quite, as we shall see). People speak to get things done, to find things out; and what can be thus attained or attempted is quite strictly codified. Hence, in part at least, the great readiness of the characters to characterize and judge each other's utterances as "singular" or "extraordinary," as made "prettily and simply," as showing "easy unaffected self-reliance," "warmth and feeling," or "passionate enthusiasm," or conversely as conveying "glib cynicism." The fullest and most outrageous act of assessment is Fosco's judgment of Marion's diary, which is worthy of a newspaper reviewer: "I can lay my hand on my heart, and declare that every page has charmed, refreshed and delighted me" (358). Language usually conveys moral status (though what it has conveyed to Fosco is an aesthetic or erotic charm); and morality is constantly open to assessment in the world of Wilkie Collins.

This functionality of language, one may note, is reflected in Collins' feeling for professional languages. Here and in other works, the voices of the lawyer and the doctor are prominent in the texture of the novel, and they are caught with convincing mimetism. There are lapses, notably in *The Moonstone*, where a lawyer ostentatiously says, "In our legal phrase, you have proved your case" (*M*, 481). But the idea of "having a case," which Walter Hartright discusses at length with his lawyer, Kyrle (461), is a crucial and revealing one. Proof is what matters to Collins' characters, and the character in another novel who exclaims, "I am armed at all points with proofs; I bristle from head to foot with proofs" (*NN*, 449) might well be speaking for the author. Specifically, in *The Woman in White*, proof is what authenticates the private domain. Toward the end of the novel, Walter, Laura, and Marion are living in affectionate isolation in the East End; the sense is of a small domestic community warmly united around the shared activities of earning a living. This community, however, is not self-sufficient. Its members can only be fully themselves if restored to their true social position, the social position that depends on Laura's being publicly known as Lady Glyde. But it is thought that Lady Glyde is dead; the end of the story is the effort to prove that the person who has died is, in fact, Anne Catherick and not Laura. Legal discussion, the legal structure of discourse and evidence, defines the task which the rest of the novel is to accomplish. Collins' sense of the interrelationship between private love, private purpose, and public status, between feeling and social role, is acute. And yet one may feel that the codification of this sense in legal terms is a sign of despair at the lack of a truly cohesive language, of a language which would guarantee public recognition without being the special preserve of one profession.

What emerges overall from such functions of language is that the use of language is a skill (even, as Mr. Fairlie shows, the avoidance of language can call for considerable skill), and that skill in handling language is skill in manipulating people. The point is made most clearly through the two Italians; the sinister Fosco has a superb command of English and a superb sense of eloquence, often used with remarkable persuasive force (Marion rather admiringly comments of him, "He can manage me," 245); the innocent Pesca speaks a (rather embarrassing) grotesque parody of English, which breaks down completely at moments of high drama. More broadly the awareness of a skill in the deployment of language is apparent in the indirectness or even deviousness with which language is often used, so that Laura can say to Marion of a hurtful remark by her husband, "You heard the words—but you don't know what they meant" (273). Offensive as such indirectness is in Sir Perceval, it also is a standard technique used by Walter, as by many later fictional detectives: the affable and apparently merely curious conversation may be a means of eliciting crucial information. To speak at all can, for that matter, be a purposive act, as opposed to silence, irrespective of the content of what is said, if the speech is calculated well enough to retain the hearer's attention. If Madame Fosco, a normally silent and secretive character (the only character in the novel, indeed, who is accused of having a "secret self," 239) speaks to Marion Halcombe, it is only to keep her occupied and divert her from the count's nefarious acts.

A striking feature of language as manipulation is the way it can exclude real communication by excluding any real variety of voice, in opposition to the delight in such variety obviously shown by the book as a whole. The clearest case is perhaps that of Sir Perceval, who, when his motives for arranging for Anne to be confined in the asylum are questioned, authorizes Marion to write to Anne's mother—provided that she asks only two specific questions (156). Thus, in effect, he dictates Marion's letter. A satisfactory reply is received, not surprisingly. It later transpires (354) that Sir Perceval has dictated this, too. Soon after, Fosco dictates a letter which is sent by Frederick Fairlie. All this is a simulacrum of true communication. Perhaps more ambiguous are the "innocent deceptions" practiced on Laura, not only by her husband (413) but also by Walter (500), who allows her to think that her valueless sketches are contributing to her upkeep: the lover's responsibility here amounts to a suppression of information.

Collins, it must be recognized, is skeptical about the skills of language. Truth, for him, often lies beyond such skill: in the inarticulate goodwill of Pesca, in the facial expressions which "betray" (the word is a favorite one) real emotion, in touch and gesture, in silence. This explains the frequent and somewhat hackneyed remarks on feelings that are "beyond all expression," which are "inexpressible" or "impossible to express," on the "sensation, for which I can find no name" (83). Hence perhaps also Laura's view that music is "a happier language than ours" (145) and which may replace speech. The skill of language corresponds to a codification of personal relationships; but there also is a spontaneous, intuitive, irrational life to which Collins gives full credence. In *The Moonstone* he satirizes a religion which prefers conviction and duty to sentiment and impulse (*M*, 289); in

The Woman in White, he has shown sentiment and impulse to be often beyond articulation.

There is, however, a skill beyond the purely practical ones, one which adds much to the charms of the novel and qualifies the general sense of language as functional: the skill of self-display. Marion Halcombe shows it first, in her greeting to Walter on his arrival at Limmeridge (59–62), when she makes two long, uninterrupted speeches introducing herself, Laura, and Mr. Fairlie, and describing the atmosphere of Limmeridge. She never repeats quite this exuberance, though there is some similar measure of vivacity in her diaries, which make up a considerable part of the text when she steps in to relay Walter as narrator (thus demonstrating the variability of the text, the jigsaw quality of knowledge, and the vulnerability of Laura, robbed of male protection). In "running on," as Walter puts it, "in her gracefully bantering way" in these introductory speeches, she is doing a lot of Walter's work for him by taking on the task of exposition on quite a large scale.

But that is not all: she also is ensuring a connection with Walter, an open and immediate one opposed to the gradual and discreet connection he achieves with Laura. (It is Marion who, for Walter and for Fosco, is desirable for her physical grace, though this is counteracted for Walter by her masculine features: directness of bodily appeal appears to go with ease of social contact.) The performance is an assured one and constantly bear the mark of her sense of having an audience. She judges herself from her interlocutor's assumed point of view, appeals to a presumed masculine cynicism ("that essentially female malady, a slight headache"), describes her hearer's assumed reactions ("you are puzzled by my familiar references"), makes explicit her strategies in speech ("Suppose I begin with myself, so as to get done with that part of the subject as soon as possible?"), and shows mocking awareness of linguistic taboo ("In short, she is an angel; and I am—Try some of that marmalade, Mr Hartright, and finish the sentence in the name of female propriety, for yourself"). She shows a firm command of syntax, interrupts her sentences with self-assured parentheses, and creates a scintillating variety of surfaces through rhetorical questions, challenges to her hearer, shifts in viewpoint, and fluidity of rhythm. Her language shows a skill which is not just functional: it is the skill of play. It is in play that grace appears, and with it individuality; which means that individuality, in this novel, arises when the act of communication is made con-spicuous.

The point is a significant one, because the heart of the novel, and even its very title, depend on a lack of individuality, on the fact that Laura and Anne are, to some degree, interchangeable. Ann Catherick is the memorable woman in white that Walter Hartright meets on the road to London in the opening pages of the novel; but she wears white only in imitation of Laura. When Walter, in the first chapter of his narrative proper (chapter 2 of the text, 37), refers to "the woman who has lived in all my thoughts, who has possessed herself of all my energies . . . ," the reader is likely to assume that he refers to the woman of the title. It is a very gradual process that reveals that the reference here is actually to Laura. In fact, Laura's being so like the intriguing and upsetting Anne is one reason why Walter loves her, as it is the chief factor in how Sir Perceval exploits her: the duality of Laura and Anne points to a more elusive complementarity of Walter and Perceval.

People do not always seem to be unique, then, despite Christian or humanist assumptions, because what matters is not themselves but their roles, in these instances, the roles of husband and of victim. But Marion, at first at least, *does* appear unique, and the book cele-brates her uniqueness by twice dedicating itself to her: once in the tribute paid to her throughout Fosco's narrative, once at the end of Walter's narrative (and so of the whole text). Thus Walter and Fosco constitute another disconcerting pair. For much of the book, Marion is admirable for the efficiency with which she carries out the functions of argument and organization; but she is fascinating as well, because she can use language gratuitously, as an image of a social contact which is an end in itself.

Yet she is not quite unique even in this. She shares her gift for self-display with another character, who actually possesses it in greater measure and shows it more consistently: Count Fosco. Every one of his speeches is marked by a delightful self-congratulatory vir-tuosity in recognizing and defying the norms of Victorian constraint. One detail will suffice, which at first seems charmingly trivial in itself: in a secret conversation with Sir Perceval Glyde, the very one in which Fosco hits on the idea of substituting Anne for Laura (although the reader does not realize this at the time), the count gets carried away into a series of remarks about his taste for sugared water, which Sir Perceval, with British manliness, regards as a "sickly mess" fit for foreigners. Later, as he mentions Marion Halcombe in one of his voluble declarations, he refers to "this grand creature—I drink her health in my sugar-and-water—this grand creature who stands in the strength of her love and her courage, firm as a rock, between us two and that poor, flimsy, pretty blonde wife of yours" (346). Triviality doesn't matter to Fosco; Sir Perceval is reminded of the sugar-and-water as an almost childish insistence on Fosco's difference, his foreignness, his obstinate self-satisfaction, just as he is reminded of Fosco's strength of feeling in his admiration for Marion's force of character, incongruous as this may be with the practical need for money, which is the real topic of the conversation. Fosco speaks in order to claim to be a particular sort of person, defined in contrast to the insipid normality of England, and seeks to imaginatively enlist Marion—someone like himself. Something very important is happening here. There is playfulness in Fosco's utterance; there is a purposeless and disproportionate self-dramatizing that verges on self-parody. But there is more than that: there also is the introduction into the text of the novel of a voice that seriously competes with the modest, business-like, responsible and tender tone of Walter Hartright. The voice is reinforced by the fact that its appreciation of Marion's character is one that chimes with the stance of the book as a whole; all the more disturbing, then, that this is an amoral voice, a voice of dramatic gesture and dramatic self-confidence.

How this situation works out in the short run is curious. Marion herself is recording this conversation in her diary, with surprising immodesty. She has been deliberately eavesdropping on it, in pursuit of her well-founded suspicions of the two corrupt aristocrats. Exposed to a storm during her clandestine activities, she falls seriously ill, which puts a stop to her narrative and allows precisely the substitution plot of which she has unknowingly heard the first conception. Perhaps this goes to show that listeners can hear too much good of themselves; having exposed her to this very ambivalent situation, Collins apparently can no longer allow her any direct relationship with the seductive count. Her later remarks about him are uncompromisingly hostile, even vindictive, and perhaps excessively so. In any case, Fosco's remarks about her meet with no answer; they remain in the reader's memory as a sign of frankness, vigor, and broadness of understanding which no other character can equal—certainly not the principal narrator Walter, who would never have dared use that phrase about the "poor, flimsy, pretty" Laura, though he has done much to justify it by his picture of her and of her near-double Anne.

So language can be play, and when it is, it can be the expression of a free and energetic personality. But language can be authentification, too, and in this case it is the formulation of an inert design. Play-language creates a new and potentially developing relationship; authentifying language establishes a pattern for repetition. Early in the novel, for example, Walter receives a contract for his employment at Limmeridge (43). It is written, properly enough, in a strictly legal register which he characterizes as "plain, straightforward, and comprehensive" and requires him, for instance, "to superintend the instruction of two young ladies in the art of painting in water-colours." He does this, of course, and in so doing enters into the relationships that are to mature throughout the novel. The odd thing is that the reader is told about this twice: once when he actually does it, and once, prematurely, in his contract. In fact, the reader is told about this three times, because Pesca has already made clear the general nature of the job. Why this repetition? Why does Walter not simply write something like "I received a contract and prepared for my departure for Cumberland"? For two complementary reasons, perhaps. One may be because of what is common to the legal terms of the contract and Walter's charmed personal narrative: his teaching is legitimate, it is the fulfillment of an agreement; repetition of this sort makes an action public and social. The second reason may be because of what is different. In the contract the beloved Laura and her impressive half-sister are merely "two young ladies," and the painting in watercolors that is to be a sentimentally shared concern of Walter and Laura is a matter of control, of "superintendence." The growth of personal feeling escapes from social predictability, but it arises in it first. Thus we have a genuine story, a genuine novel, one that unites decorum and passion, continuity and change, public and private.

A much more important instance of the way the text anticipates events, which become illustrations of a set and verbalized order, lies in the conversation between Fosco and the other occupants of Blackwater about the hypothesis that "crimes cause their own detection," that "murder will out" (255). Fosco mocks these "moral epigrams," which he claims to have seen in a copying book, maintaining that concealment of crime is no more than a matter of skill. The author appears, outside his book, to have shared Fosco's views; but the events of the story disprove them and so become an illustration of the inescapability of moral law. To this extent, moral law proves to be part of a textual strategy, of a strategy of repetition; the point is pertinent to Kendrick's suggestion that *The Woman in White* questions how far texts actually generate the reality they purport to record (Kendrick 1977, 35).

Not all the repetition in the novel works so straightforwardly. The description of Sir Perceval Glyde in Anne Catherick's warning letter, which is approximately repeated by Marion on his actual appearance (so that again text precedes act), is an appeal on her part for public verifiability, but a rather vacuous one, because it shows only that Anne has seen Sir Perceval, which is not in doubt. It echoes the widespread pattern in the novel of documents which anticipate and explain reality (such as Mrs. Fairlie's letter about Anne anticipating Anne's astonishing appearance, and so making it a bit less surprising), documents which may be one's own previous production, as when Marion reads her own diary for enlightenment, thus seeming to turn herself into an alien authority. But it echoes it in an oddly hallucinatory manner (attained chiefly by suppressing the bridegroom's identity: naming and not naming is a crucial dichotomy in *The Woman in White*, corresponding generally to the openness of love and the secrecy of law), which parallels the strange and arbitrary effect of the dream (295) in which Marion sees Walter Hartright escaping various dangers to finally meet a woman rising from the grave, a series of events enacted by Walter's adventures in America, which he relates when he resumes his narrative (426) and which culminates in his meeting with Laura, apparently resuscitated from her grave. The procedure is one that Collins was attached to, and it forms—rather more emphatically and mechanically treated—one of the major motifs of *Armadale*. Here it is a mystic symbol of Marion's intuitive concern for Walter. It also is a suggestion that the authority of the book is not just that of bourgeois rationality, of the ingenuity and perseverance that was to produce Sherlock Holmes, but also that of Providence.

The suggestion appears, with telling ambiguity, in the dream itself, where Walter says that "the night when I met the lost Woman on the highway was the night which set my life apart to be the instrument of a Design that is yet unseen." Obviously he refers to Providence, and his surprising survival is a proof of Providence—insofar as the repetition in his own narrative of the events of Marion's dream can be seen as a fulfillment of the terms of a promise, the dream thus being treated as a sort of contract. The proof is a tenuous one, because it works as such only because the text is here fancifully anticipating itself. Marion, moreover, recapitulates her dream a few pages later (305), and the effect is different: "I felt the ominous future coming close, chilling me with an unutterable awe, forcing on me the conviction of an unseen design in the long series of complications which had now fastened round us." Not a providential design, but a frightening one, one that corresponds to the complications which the reader is getting very familiar with and which make up much of the appeal of the novel, a design which unquestionably does exist and needs no proof: the design of Fosco. If what is sensed here is indeed merely criminal calculation, the dream is arbitrary. It does not genuinely form a contract between author (or dreamer) and reader, because the sense of the initial dream-text is not clear, and therefore it cannot be clear whether or not it is being truly realized. It is not an expression of Providence, reassuring Marion by revelation of final victory, but a confusing mystification analogous to the generally mystified state in which she finds herself in reality. Its anticipation is simply accidental; it is an excrescence of the text rather than a nodus of it, and one which does not give authority but abandons the text to chance.

Another crucial repetition does the same thing. Anne Catherick repeats to Sir Perceval Glyde her mother's threat to reveal his secret. The repetitious nature of her words is strongly insisted on in the mother's narrative: she was shocked to hear "my own words—repeated exactly from what I had said the day before—repeated, in his presence, as if they had come from herself" (557). But they do not come from herself; Anne does not know what the secret is, though she will suffer as if she did. Repetition, here, focuses on the difference between uttering words and being responsible for them; the morality of utterance which is so insistent in the book is imperilled in this pathetic and inadequate figure, because morality implies responsibility, of which Anne is not fully capable. And Mrs. Catherick herself will curiously exploit this independence of utterance from responsibility. The long letter in which this episode is recounted, together with many other circumstances pertaining to the guilt she shares with Sir Perceval, is unsigned and written in a disguised hand; she can repudiate it when she wishes. She does not choose to produce a document, in the fullest sense, because her respectability means denying her past, avoiding repetition or perpetuation of her guilty self, and aiming at progress, albeit only a slow, nearly mechanical progress toward greater propriety. She proudly draws attention to the clergyman bowing to her, as she has declared that he would: the text repeats as narrative what has been anticipated in her words as a boast, and this repetition is that of a mechanical social routine with which she has identified herself by denying her more passionate earlier character.

In contrast, Fosco's final confession is the culmination of his personality, as it is the culmination of *The Woman in White*. It is signed proudly with his numerous grandiose titles; it betrays no modesty or lack of self-assurance; it is written, at length and with much gusto, before the eyes of his opponent Walter Hartright; and it contains the final truth of the plot. *The Woman in White* is, largely, the story of how this confession is obtained. Walter Hartright, the arch-narrator, has made up the text (like Franklin Blake in *The Moonstone*) from his own reminiscences and other fragments: Marion's diary, a very reluctant communication from Frederick Fairlie, an interview with Fosco's cook, even the inscription on Laura's tomb (headed, for the sake of uniformity, "The Narrative of the Tombstone," though it narrates no more than tombstones normally do). Walter meticulously, almost tediously, explains how each component text was acquired (even when the tombstone was copied). But the important thing about most of these narratives is that they are wrong: biased, partial, misinformed. Most obviously the tombstone is not really "sacred to the memory of Laura, Lady Glyde," who is still alive; it is really a suppression of the memory of Anne Catherick, and justice is done at the end of the novel when the "false inscription" is struck off and replaced simply by Anne's name and the date of her death. Walter, annihilating this false inscription in reality, has preserved it in his text: the novel is a perpetuation of error. The reader must undergo the error for the sake of a satisfying disillusionment. But there is no error in Fosco. His voice alone, in the entire novel, is one of truth and knowledge, not subject even to the passing limitations of Walter's perspective.

Briefly, what happens in the novel is that Fosco, the originator of an action, of an unseen design, is supplanted by Walter, the originator of a narration. The supplanting takes the form of Fosco's being required to become a narrator. He enjoys it. He interrupts his story at what he finds a particularly delightful point to exclaim: "(Pass me, here, one exclamation in parenthesis. How interesting this is!)" (627). And how right he is! Fosco can see himself. He does not just have Walter's normal enough narrative distance from his own acting self; he is not just brought by others' utterances to see himself in an alien image, as Marion is by his own outrageous praise, or as he has himself been on the specific occasion of his reading Marion's diary, or as Walter is when he hears Marion praying for him: Fosco always regards himself as a spectacle.

In this he focuses one of the ultimate dilemmas of the book: Do people speak and write to express themselves or to contribute to a story? Walter Hartright, in his editorial capacity, is clear that the narratives are meant only to "present the truth in its most direct and most intelligible aspect," as if they were first-hand evidence given in a court of law (again it is legal discourse that constitutes the model). Gabriel Betteridge, in an early chapter of *The Moonstone*, is mildly— but no more than mildly—apologetic for "telling the story of my own self" when asked to tell the story of the Diamond (*M*, 45). Clearly, Walter Hartright's aim is to tell the story of woman's patience and a man's resolution (33), to reveal his own character and Laura's through the events that develop them; clearly the characters revealed by the other narrators are essential to the unfolding of these events: Gilmore's correctness and firmness, Mrs. Michelson's gullibility, Mrs. Catherick's heartless pride. All these are factors in a process which culminates in discovery and so in the efficient and unambiguous narrative which Walter finally composes out of their discrepant voices. But isn't that discrepancy itself also in some sense the truth of the novel? What the various voices most perceptibly have in common (the great exceptions are the manipulators, Fosco and Mrs. Catherick) is their susceptibility to the forces of illusion: Walter's falling victim to the illusion of Laura's death, Gilmore's easy welcome for Sir Perceval's gentlemanly exterior, Marion's initial readiness to be charmed by Fosco, Mrs. Michelson's unshaken admiration for him. Illusion has to be expressed; without it there is no incident, no fiction, no fascination of character; and the multiplicity of viewpoint, the many-sidedness of fictional space, so to speak, is testimony to the multiple forms of illusion that make possible patience and resolution, the virtues which make for the overcoming of illusion through time, through fictional sequence.

Note

1. References in the text, unless otherwise indicated, are to W. Collins, *The Woman in White*, ed. J. Symons (Harmondsworth: Penguin, 1974). Other references are indicated thus: *M*. W. Collins, *The Moonstone*, ed. J. I. M. Stewart (Harmondsworth: Penguin, 1966); *NN*, W. Collins, *No Name* (New York: Dover, 1978).

7

GREAT EXPECTATIONS

Great Expectations begins with one of the greatest passages of prose
that exists in English. The sensitivity of the opening chapter, its
range, the precision of writing are admirable; once they have appreci-
ated it few readers, surely, can forget it; the shadow of anxiety, concern, and wonder that it throws over the rest of the book is a crucial
factor in the significance of the whole. Much of the significance of
these opening pages lies in their concern with an origin, namely that
of the sensibility, which is responsible for the book we are about to
read. The starting point of the novel is the narrator's first coming to
consciousness, his "first most vivid and broad impression of the identity of things" (35);[1] and it is already a sign of the profundity of
Dickens' feeling for writing that he is so conscious of the interpene-
tration of sensibility and expression that he seeks to trace both back
to a common root.

Pip's self originates in his childhood, not in his family. That is
what the second paragraph tells us. He knows his father and mother,
and his five infant brothers, only through their tombstones, only as
texts to be read and which provoke imagination. Language is associated with death. The novel starts with the death of his biological
parents; its climax will include the death of his substitute parents,
Magwitch and Miss Havisham. The theme of loss or distortion of
parenthood is of vital importance in the novel; it is almost as if by
telling his story Pip is asserting a continuity within his life that does
not exist as between his life and that of his parents. In the course of
the story, the true biological parentage of another important character, Miss Havisham's adopted daughter Estella, the object of Pip's
passionate attachment, will be discovered but then suppressed, as a
subject of disgrace. In this novel, the biological origins of characters
clearly are the center of an unhappy preoccupation, at once the subject of curiosity and liable to shame and distaste; in this they intrigu-

ingly parallel the question of the origins of Pip's mysterious fortune. Origins are both part of a person's nature and something alien to it; the novel explores that ambiguity with delicacy and often with much discomfort.

The narrator Pip's first impression, the origin of his selfhood, as he recounts it, is striking in three ways: in his meditative coming to terms with space and time; in the brusque intrusion of an invasive action—in the form of an intrusive communication with another person, the criminal Magwitch (who, though Pip does not realize it for a long time, will be the origin of his fortune, and so of the social transformation that makes up the essential story of the novel); and in the modulation in the person of Magwitch from mere brusqueness to a theatrical self-display—almost, one might feel, to a theatrical self-creation. Magwitch exists insofar as he speaks, at least in the eyes of the young Pip, who himself speaks only in passive response and is conscious of his existence in terms of feelings and observations. These three dimensions imply an important balance in the author's attitudes to language and communication; they show him to be aware of language as both private and public, as both continuous state and sudden event; and these dichotomies—obvious enough in themselves—are given clear and moving form in his writing.

The writing of the opening meditative sequence is particularly superb: the slow, delicately varied rhythm and the powerfully organized syntax which creates it bind complex sense experiences of space, color, and cold together with the intellectual apprehension of distance and movement; and they further seem to enact the process of recession of spatial awareness, of an ordering of sparse observations. Discomfort and poverty of perception bring beauty of formulation; the passively observing and suffering Pip of childhood will become the skilled writer, the mature Pip who can communicate to his readers the transmuted experience of the past. It is transmuted because it is expressed: the child Pip, we are expressly told, is only shivers, fear, and a knowledge of names; the organizing mind is that of the adult. The continuity of selfhood, questioned by much of the overall structure of events in the novel, is asserted in the texture of the writing, but it is shown that continuity allows for maturing, that mere passivity can develop into shaping expression after the shift from living to writing has come. In other words, the *discourse* of the writer, in Benveniste's terms, can subsume the lived experience that constitutes his *story* (Benveniste 1966, 238; cf. Chatman 1978).

Pip's first self-expression within the events of the story, is when he starts to cry. His knowledge of the identity of things is one of distinctness and opposition; but now he meets, for the first time, with another voice, another consciousness, and it appears as brusque and aggressive intrusion: "'Hold your noise!' cried a terrible voice." The first spoken words in the novel threaten to silence the narrator himself. At least he is reduced, for the next four pages, to a negative image of the terrible Magwitch; the initiative in the text at this point, what drives on the story telling and fascinates the reader, is the voice of the convict. This voice is very different from the meditative self-knowledge of the adult Pip whom it has interrupted. It is a voice of violence and need. It is, very clearly, the voice of events and of story, rather than one of reflection, commentary, discourse.

The structure of *Great Expectations* lies in the discovery that the later apparent intrusion of Magwitch into Pip's sophisticated London life is not really an intrusion at all, that the easy order he disrupts is one within which he has rights; it is a discovery of interconnectedness and dependency. But the discovery can be made only if Magwitch is first pictured as an extraneous force, as a challenge.

His language displays his separateness from Pip and from the reader. It is a substandard language,[2] with deviant pronunciation and syntax ("pint," "wittles," "partickler"; "let to live," "them wittles," "any person sumever"); it is a language of aggression, with threats, imperatives, and brusque, unprepared questions; it uses imprecations and abusive forms of address; it presents an image of the speaker as a cannibal, and finally as a wish to be a frog or an eel. It maintains an insistent, demanding and dominating intimacy—repeating questions, emphasizing the imperatives by parallel phrasing, describing the hearer to himself, repeatedly calling on the hearer to "lookee here," requiring him to swear obedience, contemptuously or despairingly rejecting his attempt at a polite farewell. This is a language of control or coercion, so forceful it exceeds the bounds of any voluntary social intercourse. And it is successful. Pip adopts the *complementary* role, in Bateson's terms (Bateson 1973, 41–42); he reciprocates in the way that Magwitch must wish. Magwitch is dominant, demanding, irrational; Pip is subservient (addressing him as "sir," as he will later be embarrassed to be addressed in turn as "sir" by Joe Gargery), polite, compliant, and informative. Coercion, we learn, works. People— those as sensitive or as gentlemanly as Pip, at least—do accept the part imposed on them. What matters in conversation is to have the initiative and to use it hard.

This initial intrusion is one that will have a major impact on the narrator and is most clearly seen in that it gives him his name. The name imposed upon him is one which becomes significant during the episode about to be narrated, the episode of the first impression of identity. It is the name by which he is addressed in the hearing of the convict Magwitch, whom he has fearfully succoured, and it is Magwitch who proves to be his benefactor. The name commemorates a moment of terror, anxiety, and pathos for Magwitch, at least, but Pip himself doesn't make the required association. Through his name, Pip becomes a sign of his own past, but a sign to which he himself is blind. He is renamed later by his new friend Herbert Pocket. He is named Handel, after the composer of the "Harmonious Blacksmith," as a reminder that he was first brought up to be a blacksmith. This renaming is a useful plot device; it ensures that the convict who has acted as a messenger for Magwitch cannot identify Pip on meeting him again (250)—in other words, it effectively disguises Pip the criminal's accomplice, whereas Magwitch's own attempts later in the novel to disguise his criminal character are to prove ineffective. More important, this, too, is a sign of the past, but is it one that Pip recognizes and accepts. It is a sign of a different view of the past: whereas Magwitch chooses to preserve the Pip who betrays his sister's authority to aid the convict, the social outsider, Herbert opts for the natural Pip who has not yet betrayed the affection of his brother-in-law, the blacksmith Joe Gargery, in order to become an outsider to his class under the stimulus of Herbert's relative Miss Havisham. Magwitch, the true benefactor, insists on the act which he hopes to repay by his generosity in making Pip a gentleman; Herbert, within the ambit of Miss Havisham, whom Pip wrongly takes to be the benefactor, insists on his spontaneous friendship with the untransformed Pip. David Copperfield, the hero of the other Dickens novel in autobiographical form, is even more malleable in naming: he is David Copperfield, Daisy, Doady, Davey, Trotwood. Names display and perpetuate our relationships with those who give them to us; what emerges in David Copperfield is that the self underlying the name is oddly impalpable.

But there is more to Magwitch than mere intrusiveness. Toward the end of the scene, there emerges a new aspect of his speech. It is this sort of language: "Now, I ain't alone, as you may think I am.

There's a young man hid with me, in comparison with which young man I am a Angel. That young man hears the words I speak. That young man has a secret way pecooliar to himself, of getting at a boy, and at his heart, and at his liver" (38). There is quite a lot more of this, which is part of the point. Magwitch has started to be expansive. It would no doubt be excessive, or at least a simplification, to say that here he is enjoying his speech; but at least he is constructing it with an eye to persuasive effect. The language alone must convince, and not just because of the intimidating physical presence of the speaker. This is so, of course, for practical reasons: Magwitch has to ensure that his speech will be effective in his absence, so that Pip does steal a file and victuals for him from his home and doesn't just report him as an escaped convict, as a respectable boy ought to (once again, as with the lost parents, language is a substitute for physical presence).

In order to have this inherent convincingness, the language must change. It now shows respect for logical progression ("Now") and for the hearer's preceding belief; it characterizes the speaker ("a Angel"); it attains, through excessive repetition, a strongly marked textual cohesion in evoking the absent young man; it shows awareness of the relation of speech and hearing, or overhearing. It attains a menacing generality (it is not just Pip that is to be the victim, but "a boy"); it touches grotesquely on the themes of secrecy, individuality (or peculiarity), and privacy that are prominent in the novel, as in so many nineteenth-century novels; in the driving rhythm of the final words quoted, created by the repeated "and" and the unnecessary "at," it mimics the driving home of a threat by repetition. All this means that this passage brings out fully what we mean when we think of "roles" or "parts" in conversation, because this is a theatrical language. It is easy to speak of Dickens' theatricality, or of the vitality of his language, after so many critics have done so. Such things as the motif of Wopsle's absurd acting career in this novel give full justification for such remarks. However, perhaps here we can say something more precise: this is a language which displays conspicuously the speaker's consciousness of the act of utterance, of the character and relationship of speaker and hearer. It is a language which combines a disconcerting concreteness with hints of a very pertinent sense of what personality amounts to (here it amounts to "getting at"—to a penetration of the body that parallels the threatened intrusion of the young man into the boy's bed or the actual intrusion of

Magwitch into Pip's life). It is a rhetorical language, which illustrates forcefully Sucksmith's insight that for Dickens, character can *be* rhetoric (Sucksmith 1970, 250).

All this is creative; the young man so obsessively and ostentatiously depicted is a fiction. Pip does not recognize this, because for him the utterance is still primarily an intimidation, and he continues for some time in mortal terror of Magwitch and his young man. But readers recognize the fictionality of such language and a sort of poetic greatness in it: they see a helpless and desperate man inventing help and hope through the power of language. They witness imaginative power compensating for social destitution. And the events of the novel go some way to endorsing Magwitch's fabrication. Returning with the food and the files, Pip does see a young man, whom he naturally takes to be the one Magwitch has described. He is literally wrong, but perhaps not wholly wrong, because we find by the end of the novel that compared with this young man, Magwitch is quite angelic, and he does pursue Magwitch with something like the unremitting inescapability that Magwitch has attributed to his own creation. The text (like other Dickens novels) is one that grows imaginatively richer by frequent introduction of new characters; Magwitch's speech, with its comparative richness in syntax and rhetoric, is a sample of how fictitious life can be invented.

By the end of this first chapter, then, two crucial dichotomies in the use of language have been foregrounded. The unifying and self-aware language of comment has been opposed to the conflictual language of immediate action; and the language of direct domination, confined to the immediate event, has been opposed to the language of rhetorical display and persuasion which reaches beyond the immediate to form a lasting impression. It impresses Pip, who sees it as part of his knowledge of identities, as part of a structure in which he is made anxious and placed under an obligation by the use of an alien language. It also makes an impression upon the readers, who see it as presenting vitality and need in an admiring spirit which competes with the text's basic standpoint of knowledge and harmony.

Pip soon meets another language that will disrupt his life in another way. Magwitch's creative use of language corresponds to the energy of his character and anticipates his economic success in Australia: he is a hyperbolic form of the lower-class availability for work that makes for upward mobility, and to that extent he typifies a major trend of nineteenth-century society, plentifully illustrated elsewhere in Dickens: Rouncewell in *Bleak House,* Boffin in *Our Mutual Friend.* But Pip also will be exposed to a hyperbolic form of another prominent feature of nineteenth-century life, as Dickens sees it, one illustrated by Sir Lester Dedlock in *Bleak House* or the Barnacles in *Little Dorrit:* upper-class inertia. Miss Havisham, abandoned on her wedding day, has excluded change ever since; she has stopped her clocks and allowed her house to decay and get dusty; she accepts an "arrest of everything" (90). But she has adopted Estella, and she invites Pip to play with her. We eventually discover that this is part of a plot to use Estella's beauty and fascinating personality to gain revenge on men; it is part of a preoccupation with a traumatic past, her vengefulness contrasting with Magwitch's gratitude. Her language toward Pip is not, in some ways, all that different from Magwitch's: it, too, is marked by curt imperatives and questions (including the magnificently impractical command "Play," 88). Pip is similarly compliant, though ready for a moment to disobey and to politely account for his disobedience.

But Miss Havisham doesn't rise to Magwitch's inventions. Her concern is with self-analysis (and so she reminds Pip of the "young man"—by referring to her own heart) and with creating a frustrating form of intercourse (so she embarrasses and involves Pip by getting him to call out to Estella by name, although she is "neither visible nor responsive," 89). Estella herself has the superbly effective tactic of audibly commenting on Pip's lower-class appearance and manner, in the third person but in his presence, including the neat sociolinguistic observation of class-dialect: "He calls the knaves, Jacks, this boy!" (90). (Here Pip's English is judged substandard, though substandard forms are not otherwise apparent.) The gentlemanliness to which Pip will be introduced is, as Gilmour tellingly comments (Gilmour 1981, 109), based upon an exclusion, for all its moral claims, separating gentleman from nongentleman; Pip painfully feels such exclusiveness in the language of Estella and Miss Havisham and will come to practice a like exclusiveness himself.

The response of the reader is likely to be unsympathetic to Estella and Miss Havisham, but Pip's response is more complex and is a very important one. He repeats Estella's words, to himself and to Joe Gargery; he becomes aware of himself as an outsider, from the point of view of Satis House, and so makes himself an outsider of Joe's forge. He expresses the point very clearly in a conversation with the village school teacher, Biddy: "what would it signify to me, being

coarse and common, if nobody had told me so!" (155). Estella's contempt for Pip is infectious (90); the shame he feels at his family,
which sets him apart from them, comes from his repeating Estella's
words, a repetition which may itself be seen as an arrest of everything, an acceptance of the static world of Miss Havisham.

Pip then is alienated from his sister, with her bullying manner, an
from his brother-in-law, whose good nature produces an inarticulacy
verging on the imbecile. There is a class of Dickensian characters
who are satisfied with mere presence; the only meaning they have
to communicate is their satisfaction at being there with their interlocutor, and their language shows a corresponding poverty. In London, Pip will meet Wemmick's Aged Parent who, being stone deaf,
can be communicated with only by means of strenuous nodding, but
who is nonetheless proud and contented. In Joe he has a friend whose
affection is largely conveyed through a series of fumbled approaches
to establishing communication ("which I meantersay, Pip") and a
restricted range of repetitious expressions of anxiety or enjoyment
("such larks!"). This is phatic communion on a minimal level. Its
essential drawback is that it allows no progression in character or
relationship (though Joe, one must note, does gradually master language, as in his quite articulate explanation of his failure to defend
Pip from his sister [80] and in his learning to read and write from
Biddy, whom he marries eventually). Dickens does not treat Joe's
limited speech with the same contempt or embarrassment that Pip
feels. Contentment and good humor obviously are genuine values for
Dickens; what he shows about them through Joe Gargery is that they
are not conducive to the production of language or to the creation of
events or of novels. Characteristically, it is Joe Gargery who puts the
case against social mobility, asking "whether common ones as to callings and earnings . . . might be the better of continuing for to keep
company with common ones, instead of going out to play with uncommon ones" (100). The query is put inconclusively, and it has little
effect on Pip, who is committed already to the uncommon. If the
implied advice were followed, there would be no expectations and
no story. It remains with the reader as a sort of challenge, as a voice
from outside the literary world—as indicated by the dialect pronunciation, the awkward repetitions, the over-restricted conception of
"going out to play"—a voice which formulates one idea quite tellingly, in "callings and earnings," and grasps vaguely at a more important one in "the better of." The phrase ought to combine a sense

of security and a respect for integrity; but the combination is too facile, the honesty too naive, for the case to be fully made. Joe's words allow the reader a nostalgia for unreflective, inarticulate rightness; but they can't elevate such simplicity to the point where it might participate in a real debate or become a standard by which to judge Pip's later discovery of an uncommon life, of a life which he can share fully with no one.

Dickens, in any case, shows that this inarticulacy is not only innocent. It takes terrifying form in the figure of Orlick, whose language consists only of diffuse threats, so that his very name is an affront (188). There also is the emissary from Magwitch, who under an irrelevant surface of loquacious bonhomie really only has one thing to communicate, which he does in silence, through a fine incongruous, almost surrealistic gesture; he conveys simply that he *is* an emissary from Magwitch, and he does so by stirring his rum with a file. The act of communication indicates only that communication is going on.

Pip, moreover, is to lose the sense of community. In place of the warm uninformativeness of Joe, he finds the world of Wemmick and Jaggers, a world in which information is rigorously controlled, in which speech is a cause of tension, so that Wemmick has to "screw himself up" to the act of talking with Jaggers (404). Wemmick and Jaggers both (symptomatically, perhaps, of an urban and professional society) radically divide private life from public; blatantly and amusingly in the case of Wemmick, whose private home is a Gothic fantasy with a drawbridge which "cuts off communication" from the outside world. They are "split men," in Mrs. Leavis's very pertinent phrase (Leavis 1971, 191,366), and are uneasy when Pip's intervention forces them to recognize each other as having private selves. Pip's public challenge to Wemmick to act with the full integrity of his private self is perhaps one of his boldest and most honest acts; it arises from a wish for openness about Estella's parentage, from a wish to give her the continuity in life that he himself lacks, and from a sense that Jaggers, the lawyer who regards information as property to be acquired and hoarded, can only be communicated with through the intercession of his aid Wemmick. Wemmick has already stressed the indirectness of contact in his dealings with the Newgate prisoners, who can ask him questions they would not dare to put to Jaggers himself; two of Dickens' great preoccupations come together—imprisonment and impeded communication. Jaggers stresses his own role as intermediary between Pip and the anonymous benefactor: he is the agent, the benefactor is the fountainhead (307); the communication moreover is to be one way: in response to Pip's decorous and humane wish to express gratitude to the benefactor, Jaggers has a crude reply: "'I am not paid, Pip,' said he, coolly, 'to carry your words to anyone'" (307). The benefaction is itself, ultimately, an act of control. It reduces Pip to an agent and a commodity (an agent because he has to live out gentlemanliness on behalf of Magwitch, as Estella lives out seductiveness on behalf of Miss Havisham; and a commodity because he believes the status that has transformed him has been bought) and Jaggers, with his usual lucidity, is aware that to be an agent and a commodity is normal in the sophisticated world. His control of knowledge is manifest, too, in his frequent interrogations of Pip (echoing the more gratuitous and absurd arithmetical interrogations of Pumblechook). There are few books in which conversation is so dominated by the pattern of question and answer, and it is a sign of release and intimacy when, as between Pip and Biddy (302), the questioning is not one-sided. Jaggers' interrogations prove to be devised to impose a preconceived, and sometimes fictitious, notion of the situation under discussion, and to do without explicit commitment.

The technique is displayed with conspicuous skill in the conversation in which he compels Pip to speak as if he believed Magwitch to be still in Australia (350–52). He also imposes fictional status on the events of Estella's birth when he is finally obliged, by Pip's persistence and perspicacity, to reveal his knowledge of this repressed past. Story telling is a favorite activity within this novel, as in many other Dickens' novels from *Pickwick* on, and very often it furnishes an episode of intimacy and enlightenment. In this instance it almost does so, but Jaggers distances his story, fictionalizes it, and presents it as an object of judgment and caution. He explicitly "makes no admissions" (425). Within *Great Expectations*, we find a fiction that is not quite a fiction. The author Dickens doesn't commit himself, of course, to the literal truthfulness of his novel, though he presumably does commit himself to it as being symbolically truthful about the divisiveness and insecurity of nineteenth-century society, as truthful commentary; the temporary narrator Jaggers avoids committing himself to the literal truthfulness of his exposition of the point of origin of the novel, but he does commit himself to it as a guide to action (or inaction), as being truthful on the level of events. There is inaction because the consequence to be deduced from his story is simply that it should not be made public, that its telling should be an unrepeated event. Jaggers has devoted much care to suppressing his knowledge of the story; *his* private life does not consist of a deaf father (like Wemmick's) but of a silent housekeeper who proves to be Estella's mother. Sometimes Jaggers silently displays her to his guests, calling attention to the powerful arms with which, we later learn, she has strangled a rival (and so, through crime, cut herself off from her daughter). More crucially, however, he is concerned to suppress knowledge of her, and her identity is revealed only involuntarily by her gestures, which are repeated recognizably in Estella's gesture. It is a general characteristic of Jaggers to suppress or refuse information. He is not curious. In this he is unlike many characters in novels, whose curiosity can be a mainspring of the plot. One such character is Pip's sister, whose curiosity about the escaped convicts leads to Pip's witnessing of their arrest. "Don't tell me anything," Jaggers says, "I don't want to know anything; I am not curious" (350). Jaggers possesses the background of the story; it is wrested from him (the plot of *Great Expectations* can be seen as a quest in which the sought treasure is a knowledge of guilty origins), and it is confided to the reader alone.

The reader enters into complicity with Pip and Jaggers in possessing information. The communication of writer to reader that arises in the novel's narrative is a very full one; it is anticipated in one of the few explicit addresses to the reader in the text: "Pause you who read this, and think a moment of the long chain of iron or gold, of thorns or flowers, that would never have found you, but for the formation of the first link on one memorable day" (161). It is a "link of association" (403) that sets Pip on the track of Estella's mother and leads him to confront Jaggers with his sudden knowledge. The links of a personal destiny are also the links that unify English society, that connect the scapegoat convict with the new-made gentleman and the glamorous young lady. The writing of the novel, uniting writer and reader in consciousness of this kind of continuity, is set against the exclusiveness of the world it depicts. But the action of the novel, uniting Pip with Jaggers in controlling the course of information, shows the perpetuation of exclusiveness. Estella is to be kept away from her father Magwitch, who dies knowing she is alive but has never spoken to her. The final chapters, moreover, recount the definitive exclusion of Pip from the world of the smithy as he contemplates returning to Biddy, only to find that she has married Joe (without even thinking it necessary to inform Pip, as Mrs. Leavis points out [Leavis 1970, 421]). He then goes East into exile, and not to Australia; but it is perhaps not fanciful to see him as repeating the exclusion from English life of his outcast quasi-father Magwitch, returning like him to find a quasi-son in the child of Joe and Biddy who is named after him, and whom he feebly attempts to adopt. Like Magwitch, he is purified by absence; he is changed from actor to contemplator (except that Pip returns to reconciliation with Estella; but this relationship now seems less one of desire or ambition than one of shared remembrance). In short, from a character he has become a narrator; his concern is the communion with a reader in knowledge and mature evaluation.

Hence the characteristic (and beautifully achieved) tone of narration. Q. D. Leavis, in keeping with her general depreciation of Dickens' theatricality, underestimates the range of Pip's writing; but one can certainly recognize the (almost) "consistent sobriety" that she draws attention to (Leavis 1971, 371). Pip is ironic or elegantly witty toward the harsh language of power, ironic or aloofly pitying toward his own younger aspirations, humorous in his playful erudition (as with Pumblechook's premises, "of a peppercorny and farinaceous character", 83), conscious of the time that separates his narration from the narrated events (he describes the way houses were built "at that time," 40), and sometimes conscious of the business of writing (he recalls what was "referred to in the last chapter," 400). An extraordinary almost neurotic bitterness remains in him. It is addressed to Pumblechook, who, after the opening chapters, virtually never appears without some epithet such as "bullying old Pumblechook" or "that ass Pumblechook" or "that swindling Pumblechook." Pumblechook's fault is to have circulated his own person of Pip's story, according to which Pumblechook himself is the origin of the great expectations: he is a threat not to Pip as an active person, but to the credibility of Pip's text.

Overall, then, the narration is a display of community with the reader in an atmosphere of intelligence, good humor, and serious moral feeling (of real, noncommercial gentlemanliness, perhaps); and this atmosphere is attained at the cost of community with the world of Pip's youth (though here again the presumably continuing relationship with Estella marks an important qualification). The text implies some self-reproach for Pip's abandonment of Joe Gargery, but that abandonment has made the text possible. Innocence has given way to experience, companionship has been replaced by articulate language; and perhaps this fall is a fortunate one. Pip is an outsider in the world of the novel, but nearly an insider in the world of the reader. It is his world that appears extraordinary, not himself. But that world nevertheless is a revealing image of the real nineteenth-century England, which thus becomes alien and shocking for the reader.

In any case, some measure of community of feeling, though it is one which does not depend wholly on articulate words, has actually been shown within the events of the novel. The culmination of these events is a series of self-disclosures: one is Orlick's disclosure of his crimes, which is sanctioned, in the long run and inadequately, by imprisonment; the other instances balance disclosure with forgiveness and are sanctioned by death, illness, or exile.

First there is Pip's final conversation with Miss Havisham (407). He reveals to her the secret of his benefaction to Herbert Pocket (in imitation of his own anonymous benefactor he has surreptitiously bought Herbert a partnership), enabling her to add to the sum involved and so to really do for Herbert what Pip wrongly thought she had done for himself; and he tells her, discreetly, of his own anxieties. She recognizes the nobility of his confidence and asks for his forgiveness, to be given in writing: the conversation, the fullest meeting point of Pip and Miss Havisham, in an awareness of mutual dependence, in a sense of "the commonality of human fallibility" in Gilmour's words (Gilmour 1986, 102) radically transcending the crude asymmetry of their early meetings as quasi-patron and quasi-protégé, is to be perpetuated. Pip willingly grants his forgiveness and leaves. He feels a sense of completion: they have exchanged what services they can in words, and nothing more is to be said. But more is to be done. Anxiously returning to see if Miss Havisham is well, Pip finds that she has set her clothes on fire; he extinguishes the fire, burns himself as he does so, but is not in time to save her life. Miss Havisham's final moments still involve repetition, as has the course of her life. Now she repeatedly regrets her guilt and begs for forgiveness; the last contact between Pip and Miss Havisham is again one of asymmetry, as he kisses her lips while she continues to ask to be forgiven. But there has been a transformation: the images of the ghostly that have been prominent in the book culminate in his vision of her with "the phantom air of something that had been and was changed" (415). There has been a change, a purification by fire and sacrifice, that has rendered possible this final communion, this act of unrestrained acceptance, in which no information is conveyed and no authority is exercised. The love of Joe Gargery for Pip is perhaps usually below true communication; the final devotion of Pip to Miss Havisham is beyond ordinary communication; it is a reality that can only be conveyed by symbol (cf. Leavis 1971, 391).

Having forgiven Miss Havisham, Pip next comes to acceptance and communion with Magwitch. Again it is largely through symbolic gesture, most especially through Pip's standing beside Magwitch in the court room at his trial, accepting complicity in his guilt, learning to accept himself as the product of Magwitch and as responsible for being what Magwitch has made him. This relationship also ends with talk of Estella (Pip's last conversation with Miss Havisham is in part to ask about Estella's origins, his last words to Magwitch are to inform him that Estella is still living) and then with a silent kiss and a recognition of guilt. Pip prays for divine mercy for Magwitch and, by implication, for himself. The Christian motif is convincingly touched, and it has important implications that go far beyond the tolerant good humor of much of the novel: people are alike before God in their sinfulness, whatever distinctions may arise between them in an alienating society, and this communion in repentance is, for the Christian, the ultimate communication which must be addressed to God in order to redeem humanity from separateness.

Pip himself is yet to be forgiven: he is forgiven by Joe Gargery for his secrecy as a child (478), and Joe himself reciprocally confessed to his limitations in protecting Pip against his sister. The intercourse here is made possible by Pip's illness and his shame at his former mistreatment of Joe; it is safeguarded by Joe's superbly tactful sense of the boundaries of communication: "Then why go into subjects, old chap, which as between two sech as us must be for ever onnecessary?" (477) Pip and he are "ever the best of friends"—provided their mutual indebtedness is known but not talked about.

Finally, Pip is restored to Estella. She herself, like Miss Havisham, is "greatly changed" (491), and her presence reminds Pip of the death of her father Magwitch. In the final paragraphs of the novel she asks for forgiveness, for the confirmation of an earlier forgiveness and the continuation of a previous friendship—and so the two remain friends, at least, apart or together. The stress is on an unchanging affection, concluding a novel which has shown change to be pervasive and generally painful. The broad tranquil moonlight about them at last provides a sense of spatial harmony and resolves the tensions of mind and world formulated in the opening pages of the novel. The scene is a beautifully restrained and discreet one; the limits of explicit communication and the depth of assumed trust are again solemnly evoked. There is no speech in the final paragraph: Pip takes Estella's hand as he had given his hand to Magwitch at his arrest, in the court room and at the moment of his death, and as Biddy had pressed his own hand on his return from the East. Undemanding proximity, the communication of touch is what gradually brings the novel to a close. For it is the assurance of human presence alone that resolves the alienation which gives rise to action.

Notes

1. References in the text, unless otherwise indicated, are to C. Dickens, *Great Expectations* (Harmondsworth: Penguin, 1965). The reference indicated *DC* is to *David Copperfield* (Harmondsworth: Penguin, 1966).

2. On the use of substandard language in Dickens, and also on regional dialect, register, and many other important aspects of his language, see G. L. Brook, *The Language of Dickens* (London: Andre Deutsch, 1970).

8

MIDDLEMARCH

There is a key tension in George Eliot's writing: it is the tension between redundancy and information, or entropy and innovation. George Eliot's sense for the redundant nature of much in human character and society is very strong—and not entirely unaffectionate. So it is that Mr. Brooke, the good-natured and incompetent uncle of Dorothea Brooke, the principal heroine of *Middlemarch*, speaks to her at one moment "apparently from his usual tendency to say what he had said before"; the narrator comments, with his usual kindly irony and his usual love of generalizing and typifying, that "this fundamental principle of human speech was markedly exhibited in Mr Brooke" (61).[1] Mr. Brooke, certainly, is a marked example, and the narrator's tolerance of him has here produced an appreciable understatement. But this doesn't alter the fact that harmless as Mr. Brooke is—by and large—he is also tedious, self-centered, insensitive, and inflexible; he is a figure who has a strongly established, and very favorable view of himself, which is little affected by anyone else's view of him (most other views being less favorable), and his utterances proceed from that restricted self image, often irrelevant to the conversation which is underway. Here it proves that he is about to say something very relevant. He is going to tell his niece that Casaubon, the middle-aged rector of the parish, wants to marry her. But he totally fails to see the importance of this news, since, like everyone else in the book, except the narrator and Dorothea herself, he thinks it impossible that anyone should want to marry Casaubon. He therefore mentions his suit to his niece as if it almost were a thing not worth mentioning, a mere vague accident of his own daily routine. Indifference and unawareness of the exceptional attitudes of his hearer, then, produce a form of communication marked by high redundancy and poor focus. Even Dorothea welcomes it and regards it as "rather soothing," though this manner of speech is remote from her own style. It is soothing because it is recognizable; the predictable vacuity of speech is what constitutes Mr. Brooke.

One of the funniest as well as most disturbing scenes of the novel is the one in which Brooke, standing as a Parliamentary candidate for Middlemarch, attempts to make a political speech (545). He does so in recognizable Brooke style, with his characteristic repetitions, his set phrases ("you know," "now," "going into questions," "it won't do," "that sort of thing,") and with the usual domination of the first person, the listing of names, and the incoherent textual structure. He ignores the needs of the occasion, the coaching of his political adviser Will Ladislaw, and his own preconceived plan; he is, we may feel, his natural self. But this is precisely where things go wrong. Mr. Brooke is parodied—mirrored, one might say—by a dummy representing him which is raised above the crowd and by a ventriloquistic voice which echoes his distinctive phrases one by one. Uproar breaks out and Brooke withdraws from the contest. The scene is funny because of the *raideur*, the inertia which leads him to make a public speech as if it were a private utterance; and it is disturbing for much the same reason. Mr. Brooke is (moderately) lovable because he is such a distinctive character, because he is eccentric only in the sense of giving an individual note to the complacent self-absorption that is widespread in Middlemarch; but that very distinctiveness, made up of Brooke's easy self-repetition, is threatened and turned into ironic spectacle by another system of redundancy—the emphatic repetition of the heckler. The natural self, comfortable in private life, is vulnerable in public. It is curious that the word "ventriloquism," used quite literally by George Eliot here (550), should have been used by modern critics (Allen 1966, 103; Oldfield 1967, 67, 71) to refer to her own skill in creating characters through distinctive speech; for the absurd and touching oddity of the private unchanging self that is exposed to public view here is just what the novelist exposes, with more complexity and more debate, throughout her fiction.

The view is not confined, of course, to Mr. Brooke. It is claimed that speech as such is essentially marked by redundancy. Certainly Middlemarch as a whole bears plentiful witness to the prevalence of sameness and repetition. It may be, perhaps, that it is the most particularly provincial life that George Eliot suspects of restrictive inertia, in keeping with a common nineteenth-century view of the provinces; certainly the outsiders Lydgate and Ladislaw give less sign of it than others (though the much discussed "commonness" of

Lydgate, what is common to him and his society, is precisely such a set of habits) and the artistic freedom and intellectual adventurousness of Rome form a clear contrast to it. Certainly, too, the mixture of exasperation and soothing nature which Dorothea finds in her uncle will be what many readers find in the society of the town that gives its name to the novel.

The power of habit, so apparent in Mr. Brooke's speech, is a major, and often tragic theme of *Middlemarch*. Habit means frustration or blindness; the remark that Lydgate "walked by habit, not by self-criticism" (634) is but one indication of the potential liberating power of consciousness and the inhibition of consciousness by habit. Most important, perhaps, in terms of the structure of the novel, is habit in the form of resistance to the new; in Middlemarch this means suspicion of the outsider—even the long-established outsider Bulstrode, but still more the innovative outsider, the scientifically and professionally advanced doctor Lydgate, who fails in his practice largely because he wants to change things. Middlemarch does change in the course of the novel, but only in a retrograde way: it expels two strangers, Bulstrode and Lydgate, and loses Dorothea to another, Ladislaw, whom it has only grudgingly accepted. Middlemarch purifies itself, isolates itself; the political change of the Reform Act referred to in the story is tempered by the deep conservatism of habit and convention.

The force of habit and convention is clearly marked in the language of the characters[2]. It is shown in the habits of regional and class dialect, and clearly understood by characters as marking out a hierarchized society. There are pre-established *signifiés* which are connoted by certain linguistic forms: being lady-like, college-educated, a peasant, a clergyman. Each role has its tone, marked by vocabulary and grammar. A key discussion queries the hierarchy of such roles: Rosamund Vincy reproaches her mother's "vulgar expression"—she has referred to "the pick of" the young men of the town—and her brother's love of "slang"; but Fred Vincy replies that "all choice of words is slang. It marks a class" (126). Fred, democratically, sees only variety. Rosamund sees correctness. The novel clearly tends to the feeling that classes are merely different; the multiplicity of language accepted by Fred is part of a general multiplicity of authority, to be set against the false wish for uniform authority that is common in Middlemarch (Gordon 1980, 134). It seems to be implied that

Rosamund's exclusiveness is part of her snobbish self-regard; but the discussion is certainly far from conclusive.

The rest of the novel, however, does show some important things about linguistic variety. In the scene between the gentlemanly Brooke and the drunken tenant farmer who reproaches him for his bad land management (429), it shows—though absurdly—that an upper-class dialect is not a guarantee of goodness. The passage reads like a parody of the confrontations between good artisan and bad aristocrat in *Adam Bede* and *Silas Marner.* More important, it shows that restriction of language by such habitual and class-informed patterns is personally inhibiting and a bar to full communication. The point emerges with some charm in the habit—essentially, though not exclusively, female, uneducated, and middle class—of filling up utterances with matters not relevant to their purpose (as with the "points of minor importance" on which Mrs. Vincy insists, 293: Mrs. Vincy regards language fundamentally as report while the novel shows that language is fundamentally action and needs to be made effective for action by relevance). Here lies much of George Eliot's "ventriloquist" skill, as beautifully shown in Mrs. Waule, waiting with ritual equanimity for her brother's death and her supposed inheritance: "'Some don't like so much sugar in their hams', said Mrs Waule. 'But my poor brother would always have sugar'" (346). If her brother is to be pitied at all, it is for his death, not his taste in ham; the epithet "poor" is an automatism, pleasing as a sign of a socially normal decorum in the face of death, but suggestive of an inner indifference. The person is the role; so, too, apparently, with Casaubon, who always expresses himself like a scholar and cleric, even when proposing marriage: "I am not, I trust, mistaken in the recognition of some deeper correspondence than that of date in the fact that a consciousness of need in my own life has arisen contemporaneously with the possibility of my becoming acquainted with you" (66). As he announces depth, his writing seems to convey shallowness; the impersonality of verbal construction ("a consciousness . . . has arisen"), the cautious and inconclusive negative and indefinite forms, the gratuitous abstraction (he is not writing about a "possibility" but about a real acquaintance), the misjudged vocabulary ("contemporaneously"), all suggest incompetence in choice of register, an incompetence that goes so far as to suggest that there is no actual choice, and that the man is the register.

Dorothea's unwise acceptance and subsequent suffering is caused by her inability to read register as a sign of social selfhood: "How could it occur to her to examine the letter, to look at it critically as a profession of love?" (67). We recall Dorothea's recurrent feeling of inability to communicate: she typically believes she is "on a mission to a people whose language I don't know" (51). The narrator has already commented on Casaubon's limitations: "he had not two styles of talking at command" (47). We shall see in the course of the novel that Casaubon is not only a public self. That is why he becomes something like a tragic figure and not just a comic pompous clergyman like Jane Austen's Mr. Collins, which he might almost be at this stage in the story. Absurdity is public; pathos and cruelty lie in the discontinuity of private and public, of inner feeling and displayed power.

For the linguistic inertia which prevails in Middlemarch, the pre-established patterns of communication and interpretation that operate in Middlemarch society are largely concerned with signs of status and power. This implies a need for restraint, for consideration and self-control; even quite a forceful speech by Casaubon is said to show "irritation reined in by propriety" (233); Dorothea, with typical delicacy, has "her thought which she did not like to express" (404) and "refrained from saying what was in her mind" (824). The author does not express disapproval here, certainly; but it seems to be the uninhibited side of Dorothea that arouses her sympathy, and this self-restraint is surely seen as part of the much more prominent system of imposed restraint manifest throughout the novel. Even Mr. Brooke, mild and inefficient as he is, avoids Dorothea's reproaches and "got the talk under his own control" (428); the masterful Bulstrode shows high skill (or, in the view of a victim, "a rather exasperating ability," 735) in ordering conversations so as to disqualify opposing opinions; Lydgate openly refuses his wife the right to speak on several occasions, most forcefully after her intervention in his attempt to let their house. When she complains that "I think I had a perfect right to speak on a subject which concerns me at least as much as you," he replies, "Clearly—you had a right to speak, but only to me" (709; cf. 329, 642, 700).

In this he resembles the drunken Dagley, who crudely tells his wife "it's my business to speak, an' not yourn" (431) and, less incongruously, Casaubon, another scholarly, proud, dominant and uncommunicative husband, whose invalidation of his wife's speech gives rise to some of the most chilling scenes in the novel. Casaubon and

Dorothea wake in the night and he asks her to read to him (preferring the voice of his own sort, of an absent scholar, to anything she might choose to say) but agrees instead to hear her speak for herself. She urges him to make more generous arrangements for his young cousin Ladislaw (to whom he has a financial obligation); he rejects her urging by firstly purporting to regard it as not her own voice but a covert message from Ladislaw himself, and then by simply denying her right to speak, refusing to say more than that he is in the right. He rejects the chain of communication and shared concern which she wishes to install: "Suffice it, that you are not here qualified to discriminate . . . It is not for you to interfere between me and Mr Ladislaw, and still less to encourage communications from him to you which constitute a criticism on my procedure" (410). Her reaction is deeply pathetic, and it implies something important about the structure of personality. The two fall silent; Dorothea, "shrouded in the darkness," has within herself "a dumb inward cry for help to bear this nightmare of a life in which every energy was arrested by dread." Dorothea is an energetic character; her energy is often commented on, especially in connection with her speech, which is rapid, even brusque, spontaneous, direct and open; her nature impells her to communicate. Casaubon inhibits communication, in pride and anxiety; he plunges her into this deathly solitude of darkness, and in this state her inner life becomes active, producing that paradoxical dumb cry. The paradox is significant: the cry is the natural expression of emotion, of a wish for contact; inner feeling is a frustration of natural communication.

The scene will almost repeat itself, this time in the van of a literal death. The repetition is a powerful formal effect, and a disturbing one; it bears witness on the one hand the inert redundancy of a social structure based on pride and power, and on the other hand to the intelligibility of a fictional structure based on recognizably persisting relationships. The point is emphasized: Dorothea opens her part of the first conversation by asking, "Do you feel ill, dear?"; on the second occasion she asks, "Are you ill, Edward?" (518). On this second occasion, she begins by reading to her husband; but before they sleep he makes a request of her. It is the extraordinary request that after his death she should carry out his wishes—which he does not specify. The request is for a suppression of her own personality, for an extension of his inhibiting force; according to the title of the book, it is this "dead hand" that is to lie upon her.

It is only after his death that the full force of his will becomes apparent: his requirement is not just that she should continue his worthless scholarly work, as she expected. That he wishes her to do so is implied in the "Synoptical Tabulation for the use of Mrs Casaubon" that he left behind, and this itself produces a further disruption of structures of communication. At first she meditates on her married life, "carrying on her thoughts as if they were a speech to be heard by her husband" (582). Then she writes to her dead husband: she seals up the Synopsis, with a note addressed to him: "Do you not see now that I could not submit my soul to yours, by working hopelessly at what I have no belief in?" (583). The act, the narrator remarks inadequately, "may be smiled at as superstititious." It is one of the few moments when the narrator's urbane wisdom is put to shame by the intense privacy of the character, whose act is admirable as an achievement of freedom, and horrifying as an approximation to madness; and it is one of the most radical implications of *Middlemarch* that a wholly authentic self-determining speech is attained only within the distortion of communication imposed by unresponsive authority. But that is not the end of the matter. Casaubon's ultimate wish is that Dorothea should not marry Ladislaw, and this he expresses in a codicil to his will. The result is a great indirectness of communication. Dorothea learns of the wish only after an interval (532) and after some prevarication on the part of her family; Ladislaw discovers it considerably later, through a frivolous desire to "evoke effects" on the part of Rosamund, Lydgate's wife, who is herself capable of using information as a sort of power, though in her case as a sort of quasi-erotic power (647). It is generally agreed that Casaubon's choice of a codicil as a means of communicating his wish to Dorothea is scandalous; Sir James Chettam, that incarnation of unimaginative responsibility, considers it "ungentlemanly" and "abominable" (526). It is scandalous because of its indirectness and its publicity: the unfounded distrust of Casaubon's private imagination is made public knowledge and so becomes an act of aggression, a "positive insult to Dorothea" in Sir James' words (526), because it appears to give reality to the husband's fears. Sir James contemplates suppressing the insult by getting rid of Ladislaw, sending him off "in the suite of some Colonial Governor," for instance. Brooke, to his credit, stops this plan, pointing out Ladislaw's independence and his public articulacy. Sir James' proposal amounts to putting into reality Casaubon's inhibitory fancy.

Casaubon's effect in inhibiting communication does not only work outwards—and this is the scandal and paradox of his final will; his pride and dignity, his appearance of spirituality and apartness from the banal self-satisfaction of Middlemarch and its environs, these things that constitute the essence of his self-image and of Dorothea's original fascinated vision of him, themselves entail an inner refusal of communication, a cult of secrecy that amounts to a division of personality. His are the "poor little eyes," the "timorous lips more or less under anxious control" behind the theatrical mark (314); he sees in Dorothea a tangible form of the "cold, shadowy, unapplausive audience of his life" (236) (though a loved woman, for Fred Vincy, is a positive and inspiring audience, 274). His self-doubt and his jealousy in marriage—because they are potentially a weapon for other people, whom he distrusts—become "inward sores" which he is reluctant to admit, "even to himself." "And on the most delicate of all personal subjects," namely his suspicions as to Ladislaw's intentions toward Dorothea, "the habit of proud suspicious reticence told doubly." This is not, of course, the "innate love of reticence" which characterizes the evil Tito Melema in *Romola;* Tito resists communication in calculated preservation of material position, while Casaubon resists it in unreflecting preservation of a self. The private and the public are painfully interwoven; the inner life is made up of concern for public status.

The point is made more elaborately with Bulstrode, another representative of the constraining discipline of Christianity (though one should note that Christianity is not only a constraining discipline in *Middlemarch*). Bulstrode suffers from what George Eliot calls in a telling phrase which sums up a major component of the nineteenth-century novel as a whole, "the terror of being judged" (663). Most acutely he is afraid of a loss of consideration from his wife, which "would be as the beginning of death to him" (662). He resembles Casaubon in that "concealment had been the habit of his life" (882). He is a divided being in a more obvious sense than Casaubon: he has cut himself off from his past, when his business life was less respectable than it is now, but finds that the past is, in an important way, still part of him. It is in this connection that the narrator sums up a crucial insight of the novel. "Who can know," he asks, "how much of his most inward life is made up of the thoughts he believes other men have about him, until that fabric of opinion is threatened with ruin?" (747) The remark anticipates Proust, who says that "notre

personnalité sociale est une création de la pensée des autres." Perhaps it is more subtle than Proust, for it recognizes how far this
relation of public to private is taken for granted, how far it becomes
conscious only in tension and conflict; and it anticipates one of the
most powerful scenes of the novel, the public denunciation of Bulstrode after his murder of Raffles has come to be widely suspected, a
scene which amounts to a dramatically paced and forcefully explicit
elucidation of a real self. It is a scene which, in turn, has private
effects, though here less clear cut; it forces Lydgate to seem to side
with Bulstrode (in fact merely to give medical assistance) and so to
give a "sign-manual" (783) of his own complicity in the murder.
Lydgate is thus involved in the guilt and the expulsion of Bulstrode.

There are implications for his marriage, as for Bulstrode's; the two
cases give rise to two important scenes, which are systematically
contrasted. The contrast is typical of the formal echoes, the parallels
of character which form so central a part of George Eliot's aesthetic
(Hardy 1959, 13, 139). It affects their structural character as well as
their presentation of communication; they both indicate the possibility of an at least moderately harmonious and unambiguous communication; and each typifies a type of contact much valued in the novel:
for Bulstrode, nonverbal communication, and for Lydgate, displaced
communication.

Bulstrode's wife is presented throughout the novel as a vain and
superficial woman, combining the self-righteous narrowness of provincial nonconformism with the attention to appearance and display
that characterizes her niece Rosamund. She is, in short, an epitome
of the complacent Middlemarch bourgeoise. Bulstrode, fearful of her
judgment, does not disclose to her his guilt or the suspicions which
attach to him, but she learns of them through the network of gossip
which pervades the town (she learns indirectly, that is, as Ladislaw
learns indirectly of Casaubon's will). "People will talk," her brother
Mr. Vincy reflects (806), paying melancholy tribute to the power of
prejudice and gossip. But Mrs. Bulstrode does not talk. She shows
her loyalty to her husband—an astonishing and noble loyalty, a gesture of trust not unlike that by which Dorothea is to bring the action
of the novel to a climax—in silence. The narrator, as with Dorothea's
posthumous letter to Casaubon, maintains a rather trivial rationalistic
distance from the character; her acts at this stage, he reflects, "might
seem mere folly to a hard onlooker"; but at the same time he recognizes, with some respect, both the expressive function of her behav-

ior and the unlimited orientation of her expression, which formulates her changed life abstractly as well as conveying her new attitude to Bulstrode. These acts, we are told, "were her way of expressing to all spectators visible or invisible that she had begun a new life in which she embraced humiliation" (807). Her expression takes the form of simply abandoning her elaborate clothing and coiffure and dressing in a simple, Methodist style; then, finding her husband sitting absorbed and unobservant in a chair, she says only, "Look up, Nicholas" (808). Seeing her transformation, Bulstrode immediately realizes what she has learned, and the two are united in silent tears of shame and pathos. The unity of the couple is not complete; words would have been necessary to establish exactly what knowledge they share, and Bulstrode's anxiety will continue. As usual, George Eliot does not allow total solutions; she recognizes that in life relationships do continue half-resolved and unsure, that no one moment brings completion. But the power of the momentary union, that strengthening ritual (Hardy 1982, 83), cannot be gainsaid. It is a moment of outstanding fictional beauty in its sudden revelation of the potential nobility and humility of two apparently hard and limited characters, in the readiness to change of characters apparently devoted to self-preservation, and in its display of immediate understanding in a novel where understanding is often slow, indirect, and scanty. It is one of the most memorable moments of the book, and comes to encapsulate a whole stream of concern for signs which depend on affection or tolerance rather than on the conventional rules of language.

There are significant, unifying silences of companionship, too: Celia's quickness in noting the signs of her sister's love for Casaubon (71), the silent "moment of naturalness" when Lydgate falls in love with Rosamund (335), Lydgate's (brief) inability to speak in the face of Dorothea's trust in him (819), the silent communion of Dorothea and Ladislaw during the storm that leads to their declaration of love for each other (though this declaration is, of course, in speech and has to overcome an inhibiting silence) (867). The special status of such signs comes, perhaps, from the immediacy of recognition and response that they imply. They are signs of feeling, of the unconscious and spontaneous, and not, like much articulate language, signs of the rationalization of feeling which George Eliot regards as an inherent falsity in human nature.

One may question how far such scenes succeed in establishing transparent signs of fellowship; it may well be that an act of interpretation is still required and that such an act is likely to be fallible or partial (Miller 1981, 176). But the approach to such an ideal is a crucial movement of the novel, and one which has an important implication for narrative strategy, as emerges from one of Dorothea's last utterances in the novel (880). She has admitted to her sister that she is "fond" of Ladislaw; the admission is itself a sign of a more relaxed and less authoritarian attitude to language than she had at the beginning of the novel, when (as Oldfield points out, 1967, 80) she indignantly refused to use the wond "fond" as an "odious expression" (59; but the narrator uses it notwithstanding not much later, 85). Celia goes on to ask her to tell the story of her love for him, and Dorothea refuses: "No, dear, you would have to feel with me, else you would never know." Feeling is what matters, not speech; it even seems to exclude speech. But what of the narrator, who *has* told the story? What of the reader, who may have felt with her?

If Mrs. Bulstrode's response to public disgrace is a moment of isolated beauty, if it confirms a sort of private intimacy which is outside the interchange of public life, the result of Lydgate's near disgrace is to confirm the interrelatedness of people. And confirming interrelatedness means finally bringing together the apparently disparate strands of the plot (or plots) of the novel. The coherence of the text is ultimately one of mutual dependence. Lydate's response is to ask Dorothea to intervene for him with his own wife. For Bulstrode, public disgrace meant private reconciliation; for Lydgate, public disgrace means private disharmony, which can be overcome only by a displacement of communication, by a purification of the argument for Lydgate's innocence, a purification attained by eliminating the personal pride and aloofness which he has so often shown and which disqualify him now from appealing for trust. Dorothea agrees to his request. The action has complex results. Visiting Rosamund, she finds her, in a scene of silent revelation, in apparently passionate talk with Ladislaw; shocked by this recognition, she is first driven, in solitude, to recognize her own previous love for him and then, still in contemplative solitude, her need to commit herself to public life. Returning to Rosamund, she learns from her that it is herself and not Rosamund that Ladislaw loves: another displaced communication, again authenticated by the trust of the speaker. The episode links the components of the text involving Bulstrode, Lydgate, Dorothea and Ladislaw (this is where the "stealthy convergence of human lots," adumbrated at the first indifferent acquaintance of Ladislaw and

Dorothea, 122, becomes real); it links crime and love; it links conversation, violent vision, and private contemplation; it links a revived understanding of the past with a concern for the future. In it Dorothea, through her moral purity, becomes a force for unity and change, connecting disparate characters in a phase of regeneration, rather as Bulstrode, before his fall, was a force for unity and conservation and linked disparate characters through a power-oriented system of family relationship and financial patronage.

Unity, then, in this culminating sequence, means indirectness. In this, the passage echoes many previous incidents, where communication has been reinforced by delegation. The first instance is an absurd and perverse one: Featherstone requires Fred Vincy to get Bulstrode to certify that Fred has not been profiting from expectations under Featherstone's will, a topic on which Bulstrode has no knowledge anyway. To add to the indirectness, Fred gets his father to intervene for him with Bulstrode. Later, Mr. Brooke writes to Ladislaw on behalf of Dorothea; however, with the ease and uncontrollability of communication that is typical of him and of some other Middlemarch characters, he gives his own message which invites Ladislaw to visit, and not Dorothea's, which was to discourage him from coming. More pathetically, Mr. Farebrother twice acts as an envoy for Fred Vincy to Mary Garth, suppressing his own love for her; and Rosamund writes to a relative of Lydgate's to ask for financial aid, giving the false impression that she is acting as a delegate of her husband. The interventions are embarrassing or unsuccessful, but at least they insist on communication as a supra-personal relay, on the vitality of the message beyond its originator.

Much the same is implicit in the several conversations in which other conversations are repeated: Dorothea twice tells Casaubon what Ladislaw has told her about his intentions, Lydgate tells him what he has told Dorothea about his health, Farebrother tells Mary Garth what her father has told him about her own actions at the death of Featherstone, Fred tells Caleb Garth that Farebrother has spoken about him to Mary. It is in connection with archaeological inscriptions and with gossip that the narrator speaks of the world as "apparently a huge whispering gallery" (448), and the novel does give plentiful evidence of the random and uncontrollable circulation of information, to such a degree as to show that the common possession of knowledge is inherent in an integrated society (in a *Gemeinschaft*, if the sociological distinction had been made in George Eliot's day) and that common endorsement or conscious admission of information is at least one way in which the individual personality gains significance from its society.

The crucial value of language and signs, then, is one of inter-change. Ideally, communication with others shows us other people as being distinct from ourself (and as being changeable), and in doing so leads us to a fuller consciousness of our self. It should show us "what another nature feels in opposition to [our] own" (836), and so, in principle, lead us from the "hereditary habit" of "personal pride and unreflecting egoism" (383) to the "deep-seated habit of direct fellow-feeling with individual fellow-men" (668). But George Eliot sees the difficulty and rarity of true interchange, and she sees signs and language as contributing to it. Signs are indeterminate: an earlier novel commented already that signs are "not always easy to read without a key" (*MF*, 334); in *Middlemarch*, it appears that the key is all too likely to be our own preconceived sense.

Signs are all too often a mirror into which we read our own senses: "The text, whether of prophet or poet"—or in the present case of Mr. Casaubon, whom Dorothea does not yet know to be neither— "expands for whatever we can put into it, and even his bad grammar is sublime" (74). The less is known about a sign, of course, the more can be read into it, hence the fascination of strangers. So Lydgate remains, at first, "virtually unknown—known merely as a cluster of signs for his neighbours' false suppositions" (71). And the representa-tiveness of language is problematic in general. If speech is indeed representative, as the narrator boldly declares on the occasion of Buls-trode's dishonest prayer (763), it represents not truth but the speaker's necessarily partial vision. Often it is not, or not exclusively, representative, but instrumental: it is a tool for judgment, for aggres-sion, for instruction and command, it is "load[ed] with salutary mean-ing" (618), it is a commodity (and a delightful one) for Mr. Borthrop Trumbull and an elegant accomplishment for Rosamund Vincy. It is a skill, mastered with slightly suspect ease by Will Ladislaw, and barely at all by one of the most admired characters in the book, Caleb Garth, a sound, practical man whose lack of conversation is a proof of his integrity, of his attachment to achievement rather than appear-ance (but the narrator's respect for him is curious: for instance, his refusal to pass on scandalous information about Bulstrode, creditable as it may be, threatens for a while to deprive the reader of the de-nouement of the novel; readers want scandal). Communication is an act, and acts are subject to inertia; the miracle for the characters of *Middlemarch*, and what makes for much of the sense of grave illumination contained in certain foregrounded scenes, is that sometimes the act transcends inertia, that it reconstitutes their common life through a real discovery of the other in goodwill and self-awareness.

But what of the narrator's role in the novel? The narrator, of course, is not subject to the myopic egoism which is normal to so many of the characters. He is apart from the world of Middlemarch, and stresses the fact; in his frequent historical references, in his display of a range of learning and culture unavailable to most of his characters, in his rather aloof expressions of pity or mockery ("For my part," he says of Casaubon's scholarly difficulties, "I am very sorry for him," 314), in his often complex irony, in his moderation and love of ease ("we mortals, men and women, devour many a disappointment between breakfast and dinner-time", he generalizes) (314). He is an essayist, for whom the characters and events of the story are seen as typical and probable (W. Allen 1964, 83, rightly says that in this kind of novel "we have, as it were, one foot in the personal essay"; though he rather overstates the clumsiness and literalness of this essayistic tone); a moralist, who argues with urbane elegance for and against the acts of the characters: ("Alas, it must be admitted that Mrs Garth was a shade too emphatic . . . ," 275); a spectator, who can find an "amusing contrast" (44) when no one in the scene is amused and describe Ladislaw's features as "lit up . . . very agreeable" when no one else is present to appreciate them (106). If he resembles any of the characters, it is the ironic spectators: Ladislaw, whose agreeable features express "the pure enjoyment of comicality" (106); Mary Garth, who sees life as a comedy (349), and Mrs. Cadwallader.

This voice is a very dominant one. Except when characters are speaking aloud, readers rarely have direct access to their words; we learn of their thoughts largely through a brilliantly handled composite discourse in which their own words (often in free indirect discourse) alternate very rapidly with the narrator's comment or summary, as with Dorothea's early appreciation of Casaubon: "Dorothea coloured with pleasure, and looked up gratefully to the speaker. Here was a man who could understand the higher inward life, and with whom there could be some spiritual communion; nay, who could illuminate principle with the highest knowledge: a man whose learning almost amounted to a proof of whatever he believed!" (44). The first sentence sees Dorothea from outside; it presents a silent and spontaneous expression, which the narrator plausibly interprets in "pleasure" and "gratefully." So far there is no doubt as to the genuineness of Dorothea or of the narrator. But the second sentence presents Dorothea's thoughts, and irony and unreality creep in. The first section sounds very much like a transposition of what Dorothea would have said to herself: in particular the vocabulary of "inward life" and "spiritual communion" both economically characterizes her mental repertoire and alerts us to some key terms of the novel. Much the same is true of the second section, except that the "nay," archaic and inapt in an intimate register, hints at parody. But the final section puts forward an absurd claim, shows its absurdity by the ridiculous "almost" and the exclamation mark, and rather invites us to read it not as Dorothea's actual thoughts but as an unconscious, unformulated implication of her thought. The narrator seems to know more about the character than the character herself does. Certainly one can say as much about the several passages in which the narrator comments explicitly on what the characters do *not* think; this appears most eloquently, perhaps, in a passage commenting on the limitations of Dorothea's disenchantment with Casaubon, who has been treated in the chapter immediately after the passage on "spiritual communion" as an "affable archangel" because of the copiousness and seriousness of his conversation. Dorothea's sense of superiority to him, we are told much later, "did not compress itself into an inward articulate voice pronouncing the once 'affable archangel' a poor creature" (317). It is the narrator's task to furnish the articulate voice that the character lacks.

The characters, in short, reveal the function of language and communication in a changing community, its double effect as divisive inertia and as unifying transformation; the narrator supplements their language by showing the language of a detached and stable interpreter. This is problematic: the characters show the value of feeling, the narrator shows the pleasure of telling; the characters show language as act, the narrator shows language as representation. If the narrator's style validly shows the typicality or normality of life, the structure of the novel shows its oddity and unpredictability (and the tension, one must admit, emerges in the incompleteness of some narrative information in the book: why does Raffles, the shady figure from Bulstrode's past, suddenly exclaim "Ladislaw" after searching his memory for a name? Why doesn't the narrator tell us?) The argument of the novel calls for sympathy (recalling the aesthetics of sympathy sketched in *Adam Bede*), but the tone of the narrator often calls for judgment. The novel seems to endorse Dorothea's sense of herself as "a part of that involuntary, palpitating life," but the narrator seems to maintain his "luxurious shelter as a mere spectator" (846).

The root of the problem is a dilemma discussed by Myers (1984, 241): the tension between recognition of necessity and passionate resolution. It appears also in an author much admired by George Eliot, Goethe. Goethe believed in striving (the epigraph to chapter 81 of *Middlemarch* is a quotation which strongly emphasizes the fact); but he also believed in acceptance of things as they are. In *Middlemarch* the characters strive; the narrator accepts, elegantly, ironically, with the "habitual meditative abstraction" which *Felix Holt* recommends as true culture. George Eliot does not prevent us from preferring the striving of the characters. The narrator is often admirable; but there are in him things that look like a parody of detached rationality (cf. Miller 1981, 156–57): his self-consciousness (as when he starts a chapter with reference to Dorothea, only to interrupt himself "—but why always Dorothea?" 312), his aloofness, his occasional gratuitous speculation about characters' motives, the superficiality of some of his judgments ("a pretty picture," 592) and the banality of others ("To have in general but little feeling, seems to be the only security against feeling too much on any particular occasion," 88). No character in *Middlemarch* is a voice of truth, as Adam Bede, the visionary Dino in *Romola*, and Felix Holt sometimes come close to being; but nor, perhaps, is the narrator. For the mature George Eliot finds truth not in separate voices but in communication as change and interchange.

Notes

1. References in the text, unless otherwise indicated, are to G. Eliot, *Middlemarch*, ed. W. J. Harvey (Harmondsworth: Penguin, 1965). *MF* indicates *The Mill on the Floss*, ed. A. S. Byatt (Harmondsworth: Penguin, 1979).

2. A subtle and thorough account of the language of the novel is Oldfield (1967).

CONCLUSION

Communication, one might like to think, is a matter of reciprocal exploration; it should aim, at best, at a discovery of community and complementarity, at finding what knowledge and attitudes are shared by the interlocutors and what knowledge and attitudes each has that can usefully be imparted to the other, thus compensating for the limits of the recipient's experience. On such an idealistic view, human nature, as manifest in communication, would be characterized above all by a sense of incompleteness, by readiness to change, to learn, to find ways of making use of what is acquired from contact with others. A typical case of such communication would be taking advice, which implies a certain humility on the part of the person who seeks advice, and a willingness on the part of the person who gives it to enter into the perspectives of his or her partner in discourse. Personal maturity is accordingly often thought of as the ability to enter into the viewpoint of other people and to hold one's own views with a measure of flexibility and discretion sufficient to allow modification of them in the light of dialogue.

On the whole, this idealistic or optimistic view of communication is not endorsed by the nineteenth-century novel. Rather, it is endorsed only negatively, by the way the novels display the frustrations and impoverishments that follow from people's refusal to learn, from failures of contact. The novelists' diagnosis of such failures in communication make up a forceful and largely consistent criticism of nineteenth-century society, as we have seen. There is the inertia, the entropic redundancy, that arises from the self-satisfaction of societies or individuals that are not open to change and can conceive of no new information as really pertinent to them; there are the systems of power and authority that exclude certain speakers or certain topics; there is the growth of specialist languages, of the professions especially, which—while perhaps claiming to bring vital matters into public discussion—actually abrogate the right to discuss them to certain people, and which make for divisions between the experts and the others. There is the cult of reserve (often practiced in the name of propriety or modesty) or the self-defensive timidity of many characters; there is the prevalence of shame or guilt that imposes the necessity of masking much that has happened; there is the artificial self-display (often snobbish or falsely seductive) that treats the partner in dialogue not as an interlocutor but as an audience, as essentially passive and so fundamentally incapable of dialogue.

These things develop significantly during the period we have studied, as professionalization of languages and secrecy grow more acute and as access to strangers, to new societies in new places, becomes more widespread. One meets more people; the challenge of communication with those who differ from ourselves grows greater, and people are more likely to limit communication to what they can say as public figures, with authority, as clergymen or doctors, and to suppress anything that might reveal their private, vulnerable selves to judgment. Casaubon, the timid and secretive clergyman and scholar, typifies the tendency of the century, even though it is on a caricatural level; that he remains a worrying and pathetic figure suggests that he is not *just* a caricature, but an indication of the precariousness of contact as perceived by a thoughtful author of the later part of the century. The gap of private and public is growing more acute; one's neighbors are more untrustworthy, it seems, because they are less open to public view.

What this gap implies, ultimately, is something more general than the specific social codes which are shown in operation and criticized by the novelists; it is a lasting concern with the validity of language and with the areas of experience in which language may not be valid. Many modern thinkers are unconvinced of the optimistic view of communication outlined at the start of this conclusion, which, broadly, is that of the communication theorists. They are acutely anxious about the value of language; they are concerned to know how far the two major dimensions of language are compatible: its truthfulness—conceived largely in terms of correspondence to an inner certainty of experience—and its appropriacy and effectiveness in public use. The extreme position is that language may have no value at all, that we should seek to escape "under the net" of language to a more authentic world of silence. The list of twentieth-century thinkers who have concerned themselves with these questions is immense; I might simply refer to two very characteristic works of the early twentieth century: Hugo von Hofmannstahl's *Chandosbrief* (Hofmannstahl 1951, 7–22) in which Lord Chandos discovers that language is untrue to sensation, because sensation is endlessly unified and language is abstract and analytic (and recounts his discovery in a superbly poetic German prose); and the same author's play *Der Schwierige*, in which the hero, haunted by the feeling that it is impossible to open one's mouth without creating the most unholy confusions, does open his mouth, tells too much of the truth about his private feelings, and produces brilliant comedy and a tender romantic ending. Hofmannstahl is very aware, obviously, of the paradoxes within his mistrust of language; but he still mistrusts it. Hans Karl Buhl, the hero of *Der Schwierige*, states a crucial consideration in Hofmannstahl's linguistic skepticism:

> In any case, it's a bit ridiculous if you imagine you can create God knows what great effect through well placed words, in a world where really everything comes down to the final thing, what's inexpressible. Speaking is based on an indecent excess of self-esteem. (Hofmannstahl 1948, 389)

The hostility to speech here is a moral one; it depends on the sense that speech is analysis, choice, is an act of will—almost of aggression. Hans Karl ultimately aims at a will-less acceptance of things. That is why he is charming and loveable and deservedly succeeds in his admittedly vague but nonetheless sincere love. Choice is morally reprehensible, because it means imposing will on other people. This is Hofmannstahl's vision, a vision which clearly arises from the tradition of Schopenhauer and German romanticism, but which is not without its (very discreet) parallels in the English fiction we have been considering.

Few nineteenth-century writers are as radical or as lucid as Hofmannstahl in these matters (in England; Flaubert already shows a strong consciousness of them). But the issue is there in their writing, and their themes often involve a subtle and complex attempt to come to terms with it. They often feel that there is some core of the personality which is so private that it cannot be formulated in language, certainly not for public utterance, which might seem shameless, but perhaps not even for inner contemplation, that language is incapable of fidelity to the truth of felt experience. In Jane Austen this sense of the irremediable privacy and incommunicability of the self has hardly started to develop. If Emma is able to speak to herself about her plans in a way that is not wholly alien to her public manner of speech, it is because her private life is composed largely of plans for public action and because her growing maturity is seen to quite a large extent as an internalization of the values—and of the manner of speech—of her mentor and lover, Knightley. She already is subject, though, to processes that go on within her and which are hinted at by the novelist even if they are not consciously present to the character. The characters of later novels often differ from Emma in that they live, very much more, in a wish to preserve themselves from the public. Their strategies are aimed at purposes only perceptible in their own feelings and subject to reprobation primarily from their own feelings. Dorothea's aim is not success, which would be a publicly recognizable value, but purity, a value which exists primarily for the person who possesses it and has little direct public expression; Casaubon's aim is superficially scholarly success, but ultimately the ability to accept himself. These aims are not quite confronted by the characters. For one thing they don't have the articulacy needed to formulate the issues for themselves, so that Dorothea's night of contemplation is a memorable climax to the novel precisely because it shows her as at last attaining the ability to talk to herself about her difficulties. For another, the difficulties are felt to be beyond speech; feelings ebb and flow, relationships form and dissolve in a way which defies the forms of normal speech, as it is implied in the common, analytic assumptions about conversation; namely, that a definite speaker addresses a more or less paraphraseable piece of information to a competent hearer; in inner communication neither the speaker nor the information is firmly enough fixed or distinct enough to act as an authority for the process of communication.

There is, then, an interiorization of value and understanding—adumbrated already in the Brontës, though strongly tempered by social observation and a conception of social change, further explored in Mrs. Gaskell's presentation of the bewilderingness of public conflict for a delicate private sensibility, and yet further in Dickens' view of a sensibility that comes fully into focus only in recollection and in the act of writing—as a result of which dialogue actually becomes quite secondary. For many characters in the novels of this period, the values of life are not values of community, but values of pride and refinement. They are values dependent on avoiding exposure, on avoiding degrading contacts, on avoiding the appearance of aggression or facility in intercourse, on respecting the differences that separate people. Communication is limited in these ways, because communication is not the final value for such people; what matters more is self-respect and self-restraint.

But that is not quite the whole story. Communication is not just problematic; these works contain real and satisfying communication in two ways. There is the occurrence, at certain privileged climactic points, of moments of revelation or authenticity; and there is the presence in the novels, diffused throughout the text, of the act of narrating.

Not all talk is unproductive, and certainly not all communication. There are moments of certainty, moments of intimacy, and these often make the conclusions of the novels. They rarely emerge directly from the course of conversation; they are not the products of gradual discovery of community, and they involve little by way of increase in information. They are not discursive, but revelatory: they convey a change in relationships rather than a piece of knowledge. They often occur in silence, for it seem the comparatively few things that can be expressed in silence are felt to be closer to the sensitive private self, beyond will and analysis, than are the more general things that can be said in articulate language. They arise through extraneous accidents (the death of Mrs. Churchill), by magic (Jane Eyre's telepathic communion with Rochester), by sudden shifts of feeling which sweep aside the constraints of social distance (Arabin's proposal, Pip's series of gestures of forgiveness), through reliance on the intervention of outsiders (Lydgate's reconciliation with his wife). They demonstrate the incompleteness of the personality, the way it is subject to forces beyond conscious control, the dependence of the individual on his own hidden feelings or on public events. Not all characters are open to such revelations; there is no moment of truth for Mr. Brooke. One has to be sensitive and unsure in order to be vouchsafed such a fulfillment of one's needs; and these are the characteristics of heroes and heroines in the novels we have considered.

All this can be seen partly in terms of the nature of the novel as a genre. The novel is not an essay; it does not assume that anything important can necessarily be said—directly—in words. The novel's business is also to show happenings, including those things which happen in the feelings of individuals but which can be more lucidly narrated by an outsider than formulated by the person who experiences them. It can be changes of mood, sudden relaxations of tension, an unarticulated sense of closeness, that makes for crucial changes in relationships; and these the novel is uniquely qualified to present.

Whatever the views of the characters, the narrators live by contact with their readers. If Heathcliff is a weighty symbol of the force of silent energy (and he perhaps provides the strongest challenge to articulate language that appears in any of the novels of the period), he is presented to the reader by the more or less good-humored and sociable narrators, Lockwood and Mrs. Dean. Talk matters to them, at least; and it is because it does matter to them that the reader is able to appreciate and perhaps admire the voiceless dynamism of their master or opponent, Heathcliff. We see him at a distance, we sense the difference between his experience and theirs, we suspect even that there may be something ineffable in his way of experiencing passion. But we can only suspect it; we can have no certainty—hence much of the fascination of the story. And we can suspect it at all only through the interpretations offered by his more rational acquaintances; it is common-sense conversation that gives us the clue to the imagined infinity of his obsession, so that this is in fact conceived negatively: it is what is implied in his not speaking. *Wuthering Heights* invites readers to enter into a community of gossips and to enjoy with Lockwood and Nelly Dean the fascinating spectacle of a person who is outside that community. The excitement and intensity of passion may be with the outsider; but the companionship of storytelling brings a sense of comfort and companionship to which readers may respond warmly. Similarly, Eleanor Bold is a largely uncommunicative character as befits a respectable widow of gentle birth in her time. But we know she is suppressing her concern for her father and her growing sensitivity to the feelings of Arabin, through the agreeable loquacity of Trollope's narrator, whose sympathetic and moderate partisanship gives an optimistic framework to her frustrations and anxieties. Talk in the novels is likely to be partial, bewildering, and unproductive; but the novels themselves are examples of talk that is full and satisfying.

Modern readers may be cautious about such ease and confidence in communication. Modern novelists often are much more restrained in the use of an authoritative narrator, and modern critics are sometimes inclined to regard the concept of authority as itself ideologically suspect—and not without reason; to assume too readily that speech can be reliable in some unchallengeable way is to ignore the many differences of interest and interpretation that exist within society and within individuals, differences which themselves may be the major concern of much modern writing. The nineteenth-century narrator is a bulwark against the ineffable, the incommunicable, the uncertain, the vaguely intuited, against what cannot be confessed and what does not allow for dialogue; and we may now, with a certain nostalgia at least, admire the certainty he conveys precisely because we know that that certainty is not a placid one, is not attained without an awareness of struggle. For we have seen in this study that the things which threaten to undermine the very possibility of communication are not outside the scope of the nineteenth-century novel altogether; much in dialogue, much in the presentation of thought and sensation, much that is not said, relates to what is not sayable and reveals why it is not sayable—through shame, unease, social separation, a treasuring of the private. We may perhaps respect these novels most of all because they are a genuine attempt to cope with the problems of what cannot be said, an attempt to communicate through the processes of writing what cannot be conveyed in open speech.

REFERENCES

Allen, W. 1964. *George Eliot*. London, Weidenfeld & Nicolson.

Apter, T. E. 1976. "Romanticism and Romantic Love in *Wuthering Heights*." In *The Art of Emily Bronte*, edited by A. Smith. London and Totowa: Vision Press and Barnes & Noble, 205–22.

Ashton, R. 1983. *George Eliot*. Oxford: Oxford University Press.

Austen, J. 1960. *The Novels of Jane Austen*. Edited by R. W. Chapman, 5 vols. 3d ed. London: Oxford University Press.

Bailey, C. J., and R. W. Shuy. 1973. *New Ways of Analysing Variation in English*. Washington: Georgetown University Press.

Bakhtin, M. M. 1970. *Voprosi literaturi i estetiki*. Moscow: Khudozhestvennaya Literatura.

Bal, M. 1977. *Narratologie*. Paris: Klincksieck.

Banfield, A. 1981. "The Influence of Place: Jane Austen and the Novel of Social Consciousness." In *Jane Austen in a Social Context*, edited by D. Monaghan. London: Macmillan, 28–48.

———. 1982. *Unspeakable sentences*. London: Routledge & Kegan Paul.

———. 1985. "Ecriture, Narration and the Grammar of French." In *Narrative*, edited by J. Hawthorn. Stratford-upon-Avon Studies, 2d series. London: Edward Arnold, 1–22.

Bataille, G. 1957. *La Littérature et le mal*. Paris: Gallimard.

Bateson, G. 1973. *Steps to an ecology of mind*. St. Albans, Paladin.

Benveniste, E. 1966. *Problèmes de linguistique generale*. Paris: Gallimard.

Berger, C. P., and J. J. Bradac. 1982. *Language and Social Knowledge*. London: Edward Arnold.

Brittan, A. 1973. *Meanings and Situations*. London: Routledge & Kegan Paul.

Brontë, C. 1966. *Jane Eyre*. Edited by Q. D. Leavis. Harmondsworth: Penguin.

———. 1979. *Shirley*. Edited by H. Rosengarten and M. Smith. Oxford: Clarendon Press.

———. 1984. *Villette*. Edited by H. Rosengarten and M. Smith. Oxford: Clarendon Press.

Brontë, E. 1965. *Wuthering Heights*. Edited by D. Daiches. Harmondsworth: Penguin.

Brook, G. L. 1970. *The Language of Dickens*. London: Andre Deutsch.

Brooks, P. 1984. "Repetition, Repression and Return: The Plotting of *Great Expectations*." In *Reading for the Plot*. Oxford: Clarendon Press.

Buber, M. 1973. *Between Man and Man*. London: Fontana.

Butler, M. 1975. *Jane Austen and The War of Ideas*. Oxford: Clarendon Press.

Cecil, D. 1970. "Emily Brontë and *Wuthering Heights*." In *Emily Brontë: Wuthering Heights*, edited by M. Allott. London: Macmillan.

Chase, K. 1984. *Eros and Psyche*. New York and London: Methuen.

Chatman, S. 1978. *Story and Discourse*. Ithaca and London: Cornell University Press.

Cohn, D. 1978. *Transparent Minds*. Princeton: Princeton University Press.

Collins, W. 1966. *The Moonstone*. Edited by J. I. M. Stewart. Harmondsworth: Penguin.

———. 1974. *The Woman in White*. Edited by J. Symons. Harmondsworth: Penguin.

———. 1978. *No Name*. New York: Dover.

Craik, W. A. 1968. *The Brontë Novels*. London: Methuen.

———. 1975. *Elizabeth Gaskell and the English Provincial Novel*. London: Methuen.

Dickens, C. 1965. *Great Expectations*. Edited by A. Calder. Harmondsworth: Penguin.

———. 1966. *David Copperfield*. Edited by T. Blount, Harmondsworth: Penguin.

Downes, W. 1984. *Language and Society*. London: Fontana.

Duval, S. and R. A. Wicklund. 1972. *A Theory of Objective Self-Awareness*. New York: Academic Press.

Eagleton, T. 1975. *Myths of Power*. London: Macmillan.

Elias, N. 1978, 1982. *The Civilising Process*. Vol. 1: *The History of Manners*. Vol. 2: *State Formation and Civilisation*. Oxford: Blackwell.

Eliot, G. 1964. *The Mill on the Floss*. Edited by A. S. Byatt. Harmondsworth: Penguin.

———. 1971. *Middlemarch*. Edited by W. J. Harvey. Harmondsworth: Penguin.

Fergus, J. 1983. *Jane Austen and the Didactic Novel*. London: Macmillan.

Fillmore, C. J., D. Kempler, and W. S. Y. Wang. 1979. *Individual Differences in Language Ability and Language Behavior*. New York: Academic Press.

Fowler, R. 1977. *Linguistics and the Novel*. London: Methuen.

Friedemann, K. 1965. *Die Rolle des Erzählers*. Darmstadt: Wissenschaftliche Buchgesellschaft.

Garfinkel, H. 1967. *Studies in Ethnomethodology*. Englewood Cliffs: Prentice-Hall.

Garis, R. 1965. *The Dickens Theatre*. Oxford: Clarendon Press.

Gaskell, E. 1908. *Life of Charlotte Brontë*. London: Dent.

———. 1970. *North and South*. Edited by D. Collin. Harmondsworth: Penguin.

Genette, G. 1972. *Figures III*. Paris: Seuil.

———. 1983. *Nouveau discours du récit*. Paris: Seuil.

Gerin, W. 1971. *Emily Brontë*. Oxford: Clarendon Press.

Giffin, K. and B. R. Patton. 1971. *Fundamentals of Interpersonal Communication*. New York: Harper & Row.

Gilmour, R. 1981. *The Idea of the Gentleman in the Victorian Novel*. London: Allen & Unwin.

———. 1986. *The Novel in the Victorian Age*. London: Edward Arnold.

Girard, R. 1981. *Violence and the Sacred*. Baltimore and London: Johns Hopkins University Press.

Gordon, J. B. 1980. "George Eliot's Crisis of the Antecedent." In *George Eliot: Centenary Essays and An Unpublished Fragment*, edited by A. Smith. London: Vision, 124–51.

Grivel, C. 1971. *Production de l'intérêt romanesque*. The Hague: Mouton.

Hardy, B. 1963. *The Novels of George Eliot, A Study in Form*. London: Athlone Press.
———. 1982. *Particularities, Readings in George Eliot*. London: Peter Owen.

Hart-Nibbrig, C. L. 1981. *Rhetorik des Schweigens*. Frankfurt: Suhrkamp.

Hofmannstahl, H. von 1948. *Lustspiele II*. Stockholm: Bermann Fischer.
———. 1951. *Prosa II*. Stockholm: Berman Fischer.

Horton, S. R. 1981. *The Reader in the Dickens World*. London: Macmillan.

Jameson, F. 1972. *The Prison-House of Language*. Princeton: Princeton University Press.

Jourard, S. M. 1968. *Disclosing Man to himself*. Princeton: Van Nostrand.

Kendrick, W. M. 1977. "The Sensationalism of *The Woman in White*." *Nineteenth Century Fiction* 32:18–35.

Kincaid, J. R. 1977. *The Novels of Anthony Trollope*. Oxford: Clarendon Press.

Knoepflmacher, U. C. 1971. *Laughter and Despair*. Berkeley: University of California Press.

Knox, R. 1983. "The Secret of Barsetshire." In *Trollope: The Barsetshire Novels, A Casebook*, edited by T. Bareham. London: Macmillan, 96–104.

Lansbury, C. 1975. *Elizabeth Gaskell, The Novel of Social Crisis*. London: Elek.

Leavis, F. R. and Q. D. Leavis. 1969. *Lectures in America*. London: Chatto & Windus.
———. 1972. *Dickens the Novelist*. Harmondsworth: Penguin.

Leech, G. N. and M. H. Short. 1981. *Style in Fiction*. London: Longman.

Liddell, R. 1963. *The Novels of Jane Austen*. London: Longman.

Lin, N. 1973. *The Study of Human Communication*. Indianapolis: Bobbs-Merrill.

Linder, C. A. 1978. *Romantic Imagery in the Novels of Charlotte Bronte*. London: Macmillan.

Lonoff, S. 1982. *Wilkie Collins and His Victorian Readers*. New York: AMS Press.

Luckman, T. 1967. *The Invisible Religion*. New York: Macmillan.

McVeagh, J. 1970. *Elizabeth Gaskell*. London: Routledge & Kegan Paul.

Martin, R. B. 1966. *The Accents of Persuasion*. London: Faber.

Mead, G. H. 1962. *Mind, Self and Society*. Edited by C. W. Morris. Chicago: University of Chicago Press.

Miller, D. A. 1981. *Narrative and Its Discontents*. Princeton: Princeton University Press.

Miller, G. A. 1951. *Language and Communication*. New York: McGraw-Hill.

Miller, J. H. 1963. *The Disappearance of God*. Cambridge: Belknap.
———. 1968. *The Form of Victorian Fiction*. Notre Dame and London: Notre Dame University Press.

Monaghan, D. 1980. *Jane Austen, Structure and Social Vision*. London: Macmillan.
———. 1981. "Jane Austen and the position of women." In *Jane Austen in a Social Context*, edited by D. Monaghan. London: Macmillan, 105–21

Mudrick, M. 1968. *Jane Austen*. Berkeley: University of California Press.

Murphy, R. F. 1972. *The Dialectics of Social Life*. London: Allen & Unwin.

Myers, W. 1984. *The Teaching of George Eliot*. Leicester: Leicester University Press.

O'Connor, F. 1983. "Trollope the realist." In *Trollope: The Barsetshire Novels, A Casebook*, edited by T. Bareham. London: Macmillan, 82–95.

Oldfield, D. 1967. "The language of the novel, the character of Dorothea." In

Middlemarch, Critical Approaches to the Novel, edited by B. Hardy. London: Athlone Press, 63–86.

Page, N. 1972. *The Language of Jane Austen*. Oxford: Blackwell.

———. 1973. *Speech in the English Novel*. London: Longman.

Parry, J. 1967. *The Psychology of Human Communication*. London: University of London Press.

Pascal, R. 1977. *The Dual Voice*. Manchester: Manchester University Press.

Perlman, H. H. 1968. *Persona, Social Role and Personality*. Chicago and London: University of Chicago Press.

Polhemus, R. M. 1982. "Trollope's dialogue." In *Trollope Centenary Essays*, edited by J. Halperin. London: Macmillan, 95–108.

Pollard, A. 1965. *Mrs. Gaskell*. Manchester: Manchester University Press.

———. 1978. *Anthony Trollope*. London: Routledge & Kegan Paul.

Prince, G. 1984. *Narratology, the Form and Function of Narrative*. The Hague: Mouton.

Rimmon-Kenan, S. 1983. *Narrative Fiction: Contemporary Poetics*. London and New York: Methuen.

Robert, M. 1972. *Roman des origines et origines du roman*. Paris: Gallimard.

Rossiter, C. M. and W. B. Pearce. 1975. *Communicating Personally*. Indianapolis: Bobbs-Merrill.

Ruben, B. D. and J. Y. Kim. 1975. *General Systems Theory and Human Communication*. Rochelle Park: Hayden.

Sagar, K. 1976. "The originality of *Wuthering Heights*." *The Art of Emily Brontë*, edited by A. Smith. London and Totowa: Vision and Barnes & Noble, 121–59.

Said, E. W. 1984. *The World, the Text and the Critic*. London: Faber.

Sapir, E. 1968. *Selected Writings in Language, Culture and Personality*. Berkeley: University of California Press.

Schorer, M. 1967. "The structure of the novel, method, metaphor and mind." In *Middlemarch, Critical Approaches to the Novel*, edited by B. Hardy. London: Athlone Press, 12–24.

Simmel, G. 1964. *The Sociology of Georg Simmel*. Translated by K. Wolff. New York and London: Free Press of Glencoe and Collier-Macmillan.

Spectator 1983. Review. In *Trollope: The Barsetshire Novels, a Casebook*, edited by T. Bareham. London: Macmillan, 31–32.

Stephen, L. 1970. "A kind of baseless nightmare." In *Emily Brontë: Wuthering Heights*, edited by M. Allott. London: Macmillan, 100.

Stewart, J. I. M. 1968. "Tradition and Miss Austen." In *Critical Essays on Jane Austen*, edited by B. C. Southam. London: Routledge & Kegan Paul, 123–35.

Sucksmith, H. P. 1970. *The Narrative Art of Charles Dickens*. Oxford: Clarendon Press.

Tanner, T. 1979. *Adultery in the Novel*. Baltimore and London: John Hopkins University Press.

———. 1986. *Jane Austen*. London: Macmillan.

Trollope, A. 1969. *The Warden*. London: Dent ("Everyman").

———. 1973. *Framley Parsonage*. London: Dent ("Everyman").

———. 1983. *Barchester Towers*. Edited by R. Gilmour. Harmondsworth: Penguin.

Uspensky, B. 1973. *A Poetics of Composition*. Berkeley: University of California Press.

Van Ghent, D. 1968. *"Great Expectations."* In *Dickens, Modern Judgements*, edited by A. E. Dyson. London: Macmillan, 244–57.

Vernon, J. 1984. *Money and Fiction: Literary Realism in the Nineteenth and Early Twentieth Centuries*. Ithaca: Cornell University Press.

Voloshinov, V. N. 1973. *Marxism and the Philosophy of Language*. Translated by L. Matejka and I. R. Titunik. New York: Seminar Press.

Vygotsky, L. S. 1962. *Thought and Language*. MIT Press.

Watzlawick. 1968. *Pragmatics of Human Communication*. London: Faber.

Williams, R. 1973. *The English Novel from Dickens to Lawrence*. London: Chatto & Windus.

Winnifrith, T. 1973. *The Brontës and Their Background*. London: Macmillan.

Wright, E. 1965. *Mrs. Gaskell*. London: Oxford University Press.

York, R. A. 1986. *The Poem as Utterance*. London: Methuen.

INDEX

Strangers and Secrets

Communication in the Nineteenth-Century Novel

R. A. YORK

What happens when we communicate with other people? The topic has been much studied in sociolinguistics, as well as by philosophers, sociologists, and communication theorists; but it is also one of the main concerns of novelists, and it is a major source of comedy, intrigue, and pathos in many novels. To illustrate this, R. A. York studies eight classics from nineteenth-century England—*Emma, Wuthering Heights, Jane Eyre, North and South, Barchester Towers, The Woman in White, Great Expectations,* and *Middlemarch*—showing that literature is not only a celebration of the power to communicate, but also a celebration of the need to discipline communication.

Some of the novels treated by York depict a seemingly stable society within which strong conventions for what and how something can be communicated exist. But the norms of communication are challenged and threatened by two things: the presence of outsiders—strangers who do not share the social norms or the common knowledge they imply—and the wish of characters, through shame, modesty, or self-interest, to keep their knowledge and feelings secret from others. These two factors are, in fact, often intertwined—the arrival of strangers in a community creates an atmosphere of secrecy and reserve, which brings with it uncertainty, tension, curiosity, and excitement.

In thus recording social mobility and the disturbances it brings to the community, the novelists of nineteenth-century England offer—more or less openly—a